What Are They Saying About Environmental Theology?

John Hart

PAULIST PRESS
New York/Mahwah, N.J.

Cover design by Jim Brisson

Library of Congress Cataloging-in-Publication Data

Hart, John, 1943–
    What are they saying about environmental theology? / John Hart.
        p.   cm.
    Includes bibliographical references and index.
    ISBN 0-8091-4230-9 (alk. paper)
    1. Human ecology—Religious aspects—Catholic Church. I. Title.

BX1795 .H82H37 2004
261.8′8—dc22

                                                                    2003025646

Published by Paulist Press
997 Macarthur Boulevard
Mahwah, New Jersey 07430

www.paulistpress.com

Printed and bound in the
United States of America

Contents

*To friends who walk this way
kindred spirits with the spirit of the Earth
at one with the Spirit of the universe:
Thomas Berry and Wendell Berry,
related not by blood but by commitment—
to creation and to community,
to a future dreamed and being born.*

Acknowledgments

As I reflect on my engagement in issues of theology, social justice, ecology, and ecojustice during the past three decades, I am very aware of the debt of gratitude I owe to a diverse group of people.

WATSA Environmental Theology? flows in part from my presentation to the Society of Christian Ethics Annual Meeting in 2000, and from an article published in the *Josephinum Journal of Theology* (Winter/Spring 2002). I thank James Keating, editor of the journal, for his invitation to write the article.

As I mark a quarter-century since I received my Ph.D. from Union Theological Seminary in New York, I express my gratitude to the mentors who laid the foundation for my theological inquiries, particularly Roger L. Shinn (my advisor), Beverly W. Harrison (for whom I served as Tutor in Christian Ethics), Dorothee Sölle, and Robert McAfee Brown, all of whom served on my dissertation committee; James Cone and Hans Hoekendijk, under whose guidance I did my master's degree (S.T.M.); and Gustavo Gutiérrez, for whom I served as Tutor in Liberation Theology.

I am grateful to two groups of Catholic bishops who entrusted to my theological expertise and my writing creativity much of the development of their respective regional pastoral letters: the Columbia River Watershed bishops of the United States and Canada, especially Bishop William Skylstad of Spokane, Washington, for *The Columbia River Watershed: Caring for*

Creation and the Common Good (2001); and the bishops of the
Midwest, especially Bishop Maurice Dingman of Des Moines,
Iowa, for *Strangers and Guests: Toward Community in the Heartland* (1980). Bishop Dingman also entrusted me with the writing
of a draft for the papal homily delivered by Pope John Paul II at
Living History Farms in Iowa (1979). These various church-
related writings enabled me to have enduring contact with diverse
cultures and with extraordinary people who are dedicated to creation and to community, to conservation and to the common
good, and assisted me in developing my own thinking in these
areas and having some of it disseminated, albeit anonymously,
throughout the church.

   I appreciate the work of companion scholars in the fields of
environmental ethics, environmental theology, and liberation theology at the American Academy of Religion and the Society of
Christian Ethics. I have benefited from their writings, their pre-
sentations of ongoing work, and their responses to my presenta-
tions of work in progress.

   I thank the John Templeton Foundation for selecting me to
participate in the Oxford Seminars in Science and Christianity
(1999–2001). Several of the ideas offered within on the engagement of science and theology were conceived during those
Oxford summers. I thank Oxford professors Alister McGrath and
John Roche for being insightful and personable guides to the sem-
inar sessions.

   I offer special thanks to traditional elders, spiritual leaders,
and healers, most notably Phillip Deere (Muskogee; Oklahoma),
David Sohappy, Sr. (Wanapum; Columbia River, Washington),
and Pat Kennedy (Chippewa-Cree; Montana), dear friends who
have taught me much about the relationship of spirituality and
creation, the presence of the Spirit in creation and the healing
power of the Spirit.

   I am grateful for the warm companionship of friends, especially John Downs and John Addis, as we hiked or skied cross-
country while we explored the natural beauty of Montana, had

stimulating conversations about Spirit, science, and ecology, and formed enduring bonds among ourselves and with creation.

To all my friends and colleagues with whom I have reflected collegially on the cosmos as creation, on the immanence of the transcendent Spirit in creation, and on the responsibilities of people within creation: Thank you.

I thank Lawrence Boadt and Christopher Bellitto of Paulist Press for their encouragement to write this volume for the WATSA series. It complements another series volume, Pamela Smith's *WATSA Environmental Ethics?* The present volume has more of a Catholic theology focus than Smith's, additional material from Pope John Paul II, and perspectives from Latin American scholars and American Indian elders; it also has a different perspective on some scholars whose ideas are common to both books. It is good to return to working with Paulist Press, which published my first book, *The Spirit of the Earth: A Theology of the Land,* in 1984.

As always, I am grateful for the loving support of my family: my friend and wife, Jane Morell-Hart; our daughter, Shanti; and our son, Daniel.

Introduction:
Crisis and Concern

Earth suffers from a significant environmental crisis as a new Christian millennium unfolds. The crisis is multidimensional; it is a crisis of context, consciousness, and conscience. The Earth *context* of life is being subjected to human interventions and exploitations that often surpass in extent and impact the consequences of major natural catastrophes. Human alterations of the Earth and utilization of the Earth's goods have caused or exacerbated global warming, a widening hole in the protective ozone layer enveloping the Earth, pollution of air, land, and water, and the possibility of bioengineered organisms — including humans — being unleashed into the Earth's environment without natural controls. In this context, most human members of the biotic community (the community of all life), through ignorance or indifference or arrogance, are not very *conscious* of the effects of their way of life on the broader environment and its ecosystems, or they assume that future human inventions will offset current human impacts. Human *conscience* has not yet been sufficiently stimulated to respond to human consciousness of pressing problems, even when awareness is present. People fail to consider the ramifications of human technology on the Earth, and to accept human responsibility to remedy past human harms and to reject new exploitative proposals, policies, and practices.

1

The Catholic Church and other Christian denominations (as well as other religions) became especially conscious of and concerned about Earth's environmental crisis in the last several decades of the twentieth century. The churches, as religious institutions and in their individual members, began to consider more seriously the nature of Earth's totality as God's creation. This consideration led to a recovery of the Christian tradition's affirmation that all creation is "good," both intrinsically as God's work and instrumentally as a provider for human needs. It also inspired efforts to use that affirmation in practical political and pastoral ways to transform perspectives on and practices toward the environment among communities of faith and all "people of good will."

The Catholic Church's shift in perceptions about the nature of Nature can be seen in the change in environmental attitudes in church documents from the time of the Second Vatican Council (1962–65) through the beginning of the twenty-first century. The change in papal and bishops' ideas often was preceded and accompanied by developments in lay Catholic thought on the environment. Catholic academic and activist analyses of the state of Earth and proposals for environmental respect and responsibility stimulated and became incorporated into "official" Catholic environmental teachings.

U.S. Catholic social teaching on ecology progressed significantly in the twentieth century. Regionally and nationally, numerous bishops, theologian consultants, and interested laity analyzed environmental issues, creatively related traditional teachings to them, and replaced anthropocentric and individualistic perspectives with a new but biblically based vision of humanity integrated with its habitat, the biotic community, and the Earth, and responsible as a collaborative and egalitarian community for the equitable distribution of the goods of Earth. Teachings about a "sacramental universe," extension of "common good" to include all creation, and advocacy of a "commons" characterized by ecojustice effected a substantive transformation of the Catholic ecological tradition, with significant social implications. The complementary components of this integrated vision are that people are called to care for both God's good creation and humanity's common good. In this vision, humanity will be integrated with its habitat, the biotic community, and Earth,[1] and responsible as a collaborative community for the equitable distribution of the goods of Earth. The vision is rooted deep in the Bible and in two millennia of church teachings and practice, and in the lives and perspectives of people such as Saint Francis of Assisi (his life of simplicity of possessions and of kinship with all creatures), Saint Benedict (his ideas on community and on responsible development of the Earth to meet human needs), and Saint Augustine (his call for respect for all creatures, even those not needed by humans, because they have some integrated role in creation).[2] The church has developed further the theology of creation hinted at in Vatican II, thereby enhancing the church *ad Intra,* internally among its adherents; and has related that theology to the needs of the people of God in their concrete ecological contexts, thereby engaging the church *ad Extra,* with the world beyond the church's institutional, intellectual, religious, and community confines.

Peoples of all faiths and members of faith-based and secular environmental organizations are responding to the global environmental crisis. This response includes specific considerations and contributions of the Catholic community, whose members are engaged in efforts to care for and about creation not only through constructive statements but also in concrete historical projects. This writing focuses on efforts in the Catholic Church. I have been immersed in those theoretical and practical efforts over decades; I am interested in fostering a greater awareness of Catholic ecojustice teaching among Catholics and in the broader faith and environmental communities. I hope that this awareness will further significant additional efforts to confront and remedy current problems and injustices, conserve the Earth and protect the community of life, and construct communities that will think about and work both to prevent future human-caused problems and to inspire and strengthen people to care for all creation.

Within the Catholic community, insights from around the world have addressed the environmental crisis. In this work, again for purposes of narrowing the focus of a broad field of endeavor, the Americas will be a general area of study, North America a particular area, and the United States the primary focus. As a prelude and a complement to the work among Catholics in the Americas, Vatican-based documents will be reviewed.

Scholars in other Christian traditions, as well as in other religions of the world, have made significant contributions to theology-ecology literature. Their works have inspired Catholic authors as well as members of their own faith communities. Selected works from these authors are included in the bibliography.

The focus of this writing is *environmental theology:* theology that explores and is influenced by the reality and consciousness of human existence in an interrelated and interdependent biosphere and universe. It is a creation-centered theology: it recognizes that the biotic community—the community of all life—lives in a created cosmos and is engaged not only with the intricacies of that existence, but also with its source: the Creator Spirit who continues to create the cosmos and guide it toward the full realization of its envisioned potential. The Spirit's creative imagination and creating power and compassionate love flow into this ongoing work, through the stability of guiding laws and from the contingency of divine involvement. Cosmic dynamics, biological evolution, and divine vision and compassion creatively weave a cosmic tapestry and play the music for the cosmic dance it represents: an interplay of energies, elements, entities, events, and engagements having the signature of its composer and artist.

In the description and analysis of the relationship of theology and ecology in Catholic thought that follows, anthropocentric, stewardship, and relational perspectives in environmental theology; creation as common ground and common good; and a new perspective, creation as a sacramental commons, will be discussed.

The book generally has a historical progression, from the time of the Second Vatican Council through the beginning of the new millennium, and includes flashbacks to earlier eras of the Christian story. The entirety of Catholic documents and ideas is not encompassed by this book. The reader is encouraged to explore more in depth the authors, passages, and statements cited here. Chapter 1 discusses documents emerging directly or indirectly from the Vatican. Chapter 2 looks at statements originating from national bishops' conferences in the Dominican Republic, Guatemala, and the United States. In chapter 3, regional bishops' pastoral letters from the United States and Canada are studied. Chapters 4 and 5 focus on writings and teachings from native Americans and theologians in the United States and Latin America; chapter 6 brings together significant themes from all of the preceding sources, and suggests areas and concepts for further elaboration in the church; and chapter 7 offers ideas for concrete projects in which interested members of faith communities and their collaborators might work together to make a concrete reality of the environmental theology teachings and visions presented in prior chapters.

In church documents and other texts cited, the authors' language usages are left as expressed in their work. Where non-inclusive language is used in the original, it is retained, and where God is referred to as a male person, that too is retained, so that the reader may see the attitude and consciousness of the respective writers. The present author did not deem it historically fitting to render others' works or ideas in more socially and theologically appropriate terms, even when in disagreement with them.

After Vatican II, Léon-Joseph Cardinal Suenens envisioned "a pilgrim Church, going forward step by step along her unfinished path."[3] He also spoke of the "right to dream," which is "the right to start afresh, not from what is, but from what 'ought to be'—to go back to the first, the original, the 'normal' meaning of Christianity."[4] The Catholic Church's explorations of theology-ecology interactions, and its developing view of creation as the context of the church's theology *ad Intra* and *ad Extra,* represent church efforts to walk the unfinished path of forming Christian ideas about and actions of caring for God's creation. Christian caretaking practices flow from a dream about what "ought to be" in God's creation. When Christians work with the Spirit to renew the Earth, the dream gradually will become realized for generations to come.

1
Creation, Creatures, and Community Consideration

At the time of the Second Vatican Council, there was little consciousness in the church or in the broader society of a developing ecological crisis. The *Pastoral Constitution on the Church in the Modern World (Gaudium et Spes),* for example, focused on issues of family, culture, human dignity and human community, socioeconomic life, politics, peace, and international community relations—not on any specific environmental concerns.

The Second Vatican Council did consider, from an anthropocentric perspective, a few environment-related issues, such as a just distribution of the Earth's goods, neighbor-regard, and intergenerational responsibility. This limited consideration might have been expected from the institutional church in an era when there was no substantial and extensive global consideration of environmental problems, nor of the benefits and needs of diverse creatures in interrelated ecosystems. Concern for an "environmental crisis" and advocacy of "respect for the integrity of creation," terms taken as givens today, were not part of the consciousness of the council nor of the broader human community during the council years. The council's perspective proceeded from the then-existing basic Christian attitude toward creation: it is a hierarchically structured pyramid with humanity atop as its ruler in God's image, exercising

dominion over Earth and being the ultimate and appropriate bene-
ficiary of Earth's goods, which were provided by the Creator to
serve humanity. The human responsibility to foster an equitable
distribution of Earth's goods was advocated also. The union of
anthropocentrism and social concern would be the foundation
for—but not restrict the further development of—Catholic environmental teaching.

The Council Fathers did not address environmental issues
specifically, directly, and forcefully because they did not have an
extensive historical base from which to draw insights about
responsibility for creation, and they lacked the resources with
which to address ecological issues. However, a careful reading of
Lumen Gentium and *Gaudium et Spes,* and a conscientious
extrapolation of their ideas on the role of the church in relation to
the world and to the Spirit, reveal historical precedents, insights,
and potential practices used later to address and attempt to alleviate ongoing ecological crises.

In *Lumen Gentium (Dogmatic Constitution on the Church),*
for example, the council declared that Catholics should "learn the
deepest meaning and the value of all creation, and how to relate it
to the praise of God" and "work to see that created goods are
more fittingly distributed among men" (LG §36). These words
present in seminal form the bases for the church's later formula-
tion of the two pillars of its environmental teachings: respect for
Earth and the biotic community (the community of all life) as
God's creations; and provision of steps to ensure that from the
goods of creation human needs would be met as people worked
together for the common good.

In *Gaudium et Spes,* then-current attitudes about creation and
human relations with it were expressed also. The document states
that humankind "can and should increasingly consolidate its control over creation" (GS §9); that "all things on earth should be
related to man as their center and crown" (GS §12); and that "man,
created in God's image, received a mandate to subject to himself
the earth and all that it contains" (GS §34).[1] In this anthropocentric

view, "man" at the pinnacle of creation has the right to dominate—the right to "subject to himself" or to "subdue" (GS §12)—all other creatures. Subjection of creatures is limited: it does not allow subjection of humans; in fact, people should not neglect the welfare of members of the human community (GS §34). The right to "subdue," then, is qualified: "man" has the mandate to subject the Earth and all in it, but also is to use the mandate to build up the world, in part to care for other people. The focus remains anthropocentric, but it is an extended anthropocentrism: "man" should be concerned about the well-being of all humans.

While *Gaudium et Spes* affirms anthropocentric attitudes, it does not support individualistic greed. As in prior church teachings, the council participants declare here that this "man-centered" focus in creation is to help meet human needs through the exercise of human responsibility. There is no acknowledgment of the evolutionary unfolding of God's creative work as an ongoing process, nor of God's work having a "perfection" or an integrity pleasing to God as it is, without human intervention or alteration. One could reason from this perspective, for example, that trees are intended primarily for "man's" use and for "man's" transformation into something other than what they are in their natural state; the carpenter will "perfect" the tree by making it into a chair.

In his role as a major guiding force at the Second Vatican Council, Léon-Joseph Cardinal Suenens persuaded Pope John XXIII and the Council Fathers that it was essential for the church to look at itself internally—*ad Intra*—and in terms of its external ministry in the world—*ad Extra*. From his perspective and under his guidance emerged *Lumen Gentium* (focused *ad Intra*) and *Gaudium et Spes* (focused *ad Extra*). In its modest deliberations on environmental issues, the council issued statements that, when they were developed dynamically later in evolving social and ecological contexts, began to have a dual *ad Intra* and *ad Extra* impact, one more extensive than was envisioned during the council era.

In the decades since the council, for example, individuals, communities, and nations have realized that the environment—

"God's creation," for people of faith—is experiencing crises that demand consideration and resolution. The church acknowledges that for centuries its members, through ignorance or greed, have deprived their neighbors of needed goods by depleting non renewable resources; by diminishing the quality of air, soil, and water; and by desacralizing revelatory, beautiful places in cre-ation—all of which imperils the well-being of future generations. In response, the church in its global, national, and regional com-munities has begun to evaluate its responsibilities to care for cre-ation relative to the exigencies of its historical and ecological contexts, so that creation might both meet human needs and retain its integrity as God's good work. As we shall see later, the devel-oping and dynamic Catholic social thought on the environment carries forth the *Gaudium et Spes* and *Lumen Gentium* statements cited, as well as teachings that the Christian community is guided by the Spirit "who fills the earth" (GS §11); that God pronounced all creation "very good" (GS §12); that humanity "comprises a single world community" (GS §33); that "all things are endowed with their own stability, truth, goodness, proper laws, and order," and that believers of every religious tradition have heard God's "revealing voice in the discourse of creatures" (GS §36); and that hope in a new Earth should not weaken but "stimulate our con-cern for cultivating this one" (GS §39).

Openness to the Spirit's guidance, as advocated by the council, provided a basis for theologians and church leaders to "scrutinize the signs of the times" with the intent of deciphering the human role in creation, as "images of God," both to care for a creation that is good apart from humanity and has meaning to God in itself and not just for humanity; and to discern ways in which humanity and the rest of creation might be so related as to benefit both and give glory to God. The result has been evolution-ary environmental ethics and environmental theology, which offer ideas about the intrinsic value of all creatures and Earth, responsible use of Earth's goods ("resources"), a sense of intergenerational responsibility, and a heightened consciousness of the immanence of the Creator in creation.

The developing *ad Intra* teachings of the church on creation serve as the focus for theological reflection, and the *ad Extra* situation of the church in an evolutionary environmental context serves as the locus for ecological concretization of that reflection. These dynamic developments carry forth Cardinal Suenens's hope that the church would "continue tirelessly to probe the future, to listen to its voice, spoken and unspoken," and "pursue the dialogue which began at Vatican II" (15 October 1968).[2] He declared that it was important to "look at this world of the twenty-first century, which is already dawning, with new eyes, with the eyes of Christ....What we need is a metamorphosis, a Pentecost, a world created anew in the Spirit" (28 November 1968).[3]

In the aftermath and afterglow of Vatican II, the dynamic development of church doctrine advocated by Cardinal Suenens began slowly to unfold. Vatican-based statements in the 1990s included encyclicals and a message from Pope John Paul II, an Earth Summit address by Archbishop Renato Martino, and the *Catechism of the Catholic Church*. The twofold theme begun at the council was further developed by the church: humans have dominion over creation; in exercising dominion people are to care for creation and use its goods in such a way that the needs of all people might be met. As church consciousness of human-caused environmental harms increased, church leaders discussed the environment more frequently, more urgently, and more extensively.

Pope John Paul II: Exploring and Expanding the Tradition

The thought of John Paul II on environmental issues, while based on a traditional anthropocentrism, offers key insights that carry the tradition forward: the idea of a "social mortgage" on private property, and the teaching that care for creation is "an essential part" of Christian faith.

When he visited the Americas in the first year of his pontificate, Pope John Paul II called for land stewardship and a just distribution of land and its goods. In his journey to the Latin American Bishops' Conference in Puebla, Mexico (January 1979), he declared in Cuilapán that "private property always carries with it a social mortgage, so that material possessions may serve the general goal that God intended."[4] (The pope would reiterate this idea of a "social mortgage" in his 1987 encyclical *On Social Concern,* §42.) Private property, then, is not entirely private: it is intended to provide not only for the living space and livelihood of its civil owners, but also to help meet the needs of the broader community in which those owners live or operate their businesses. Later that year, the social mortgage idea was intimated in Des Moines, Iowa, when in heartland America John Paul II stated that "the land is God's gift entrusted to people from the very beginning," adding that "the land is not only God's gift, it is also man's responsibility," and therefore "the land must be conserved with care since it is intended to be fruitful for generation upon generation" so that "your children's children and generations after them will inherit an even richer land than was entrusted to you."[5] The pope's statements reflect biblical injunctions, and ask Catholics to reflect upon the extent to which they have been working well with the Earth to care for God's creation while meeting human needs through generations.

On January 1, 1990, Pope John Paul II issued a "World Day of Peace" statement focused on the environment: *The Ecological Crisis: A Common Responsibility.*[6] In that message, John Paul lamented a "lack of due respect for nature" and the "plundering of natural resources," and declared that "faced with the widespread destruction of the environment, people everywhere are coming to understand that we cannot continue to use the goods of the earth as we have in the past." He advocated attention to issues of ecosystem balance and promotion of intergenerational responsibility, and asserted that species extinction and reckless exploitation of natural resources, even when done in the name of "progress," are ulti-mately destructive to humankind (§6, 7).

Pope John Paul II went on to note that "the earth is ulti-mately a common heritage, the fruits of which are for the benefit of all....It is manifestly unjust that a privileged few should con-tinue to accumulate excess goods, squandering available resources, while masses of people are living in conditions of mis-ery at the very lowest level of subsistence" (§8). He said that "an education in ecological responsibility is urgent: responsibility for oneself, for others, and for the earth" (§13), and then declared that "the aesthetic value of creation cannot be overlooked. Our very contact with nature has a deep restorative power; contemplation of its magnificence imparts peace and serenity," and the "good-ness and beauty of creation" gives glory to God (§14).

Ecology and economics are linked, for a "proper ecological balance will not be found without directly addressing the struc-tural forms of poverty" (§11). Moreover, for humans, "the right to a safe environment is ever more insistently presented today as a right that must be included in an updated Charter of Human Rights" (§9).

The role of war in causing environmental devastation was noted by the pope, who stated that war on a global scale would result in "incalculable ecological damage," and even on a lesser scale would "damage the land" while "poisoning the soil and water" (§12).

In a highly significant statement, Pope John Paul II declared that environmental concerns are not an addition to what it means to be a follower of Christ: "Christians, in particular, realize that their responsibility within creation and their duty toward nature and the Creator are an *essential part of their faith*" (§15; emphasis added). The phrase "essential part of their faith" represents a sub-stantive addition to Catholic social consciousness. John Paul II indicated that care for creation is not an optional attitude and activity for Christians, to be engaged in or ignored as they choose, in their pursuit of a heavenly home; Christians must fulfill their responsibilities to God's creation while in their Earth home.

In the conclusion of his message, John Paul reminded Catholics of their "serious obligation to care for all of creation" (§16).

In the same year in which his ecological message was released, Pope John Paul II issued the Apostolic Constitution *Ex Corde Ecclesiae (On Catholic Universities),* which focused on the relationship between Catholic higher educational institutions and the magisterium. In this document, the pope stated that research in Catholic institutions should include a study of "serious contemporary problems" including "the promotion of justice for all…[and] the protection of nature" (§32). He added that the promotion of social justice "is of particular importance for each Catholic University," referencing the social teachings of the church (§34); he exhorted Catholic universities to relate to and collaborate with other universities to promote "the defence of nature in accordance with an awareness of the international ecological situation" (§37). In these statements John Paul II urged the universities to educate their students about the twofold focus of Catholic environmental teaching: care for creation as a whole and care for the human community within creation.

In 1991, in *Centesimus Annus (On the Hundredth Anniversary of Rerum Novarum),* John Paul II made reference to military impacts on people and the environment when he stated that an "insane arms race" in the post–World War II era had "swallowed up the resources needed" for nations' internal development and for the wealthier nations to assist the less developed nations (§18); he noted that "enormous resources can be made available by disarming the huge military machines which were constructed for the conflict between East and West" (§28).

He declared further that God placed the world "in human hands so that people may make it fruitful and more perfect through their work" (§51). He suggested that people should have a sense of "wonder in the presence of being" and appreciate "the beauty which enables one to see in visible things the message of the invisible God who created them" (§37)—phrasing that is reminiscent of the concept of the "sacramental universe" offered by the U.S. Catholic bishops in the same year. He lamented people's excessive consumption of Earth's "resources" and their submission of Earth to themselves "as though it did not have its own requisites and a prior God-given purpose." People did not seek to fulfill their role "as a cooperator with God in the work of creation," but set themselves up "in place of God" and "tyrannized rather than governed" creation (§37).

The pope addressed several environmental issues in his 1999 World Day of Peace Message, "Respect for Human Rights: The Secret of True Peace,"[7] when he stated:

> The danger of serious damage to land and sea, and to the climate, flora and fauna calls for a profound change in modern civilization's typical consumer lifestyle, particularly in the richer countries. Nor can we underestimate another risk, even if it is a less drastic one: People who live in poverty in rural areas can be driven by necessity to exploit beyond reasonable limits the little land which they have at their disposal....The world's present and future depend on the safeguarding of creation because of the endless interdependence between human beings and their environment. Placing human well-being at the center of concern for the environment is actually the surest way of safeguarding creation; this in fact stimulates the responsibility of the individual with regard to natural resources and their judicious use. (§10)

The statement correctly notes that both rich and poor can devastate the environment, the former from greed and the latter from need; advocates the safeguarding of creation; and recognizes the interdependence between humans and the Earth. Unfortunately, it naively suggests that anthropocentrism ("placing human well-being at the center of concern for the environment") will safeguard creation, a proposal that contradicts the first part of the paragraph, which notes environmental devastation, since the latter is based on an anthropocentric ideology. (It is a kind of "trickle down ecology," with similar assumptions as "trickle down economics," which has been a historical failure where tried. The "trickle down" proposal has not worked in the real world, and lacks validity in both human history and natural history. In human history, where such efforts have been advocated, among the general public the rich have become richer and the poor poorer, and in the workplace CEOs have enriched themselves while the corporations they headed went bankrupt and employees lost their savings and retirement accounts. The proposal contradicts the pope's own statements about economic justice, where he laments the fact that rich individuals and families do not care about their poor brothers and sisters, employers do not seek their employees' well-being, and wealthy nations do not assist poor nations. In natural history, if a predator—and humans are the most predatory of creatures, whose predation and predation capabilities and possibilities are enhanced through negative uses of science and technology—uses its natural abilities without concern for the rest of the biotic community or its habitat, it might destroy elements of both, and thereby eventually itself.)

The "humans benefit, creation benefits" idea is also an implied appeal to human self-interest: humans should safeguard creation not because it is God's or because it has an intrinsic value in itself, but because doing so will benefit humankind. Finally, it is an appeal to pride, that humans should benefit first, and that individuals seeing human well-being at the center of the natural world would be more responsible.

On several occasions John Paul II addressed Native peoples' issues. In Phoenix, Arizona, in his address[8] to a meeting with Native Americans at the Veterans Memorial Coliseum on September 14, 1987, he declared that they were "the noble descendants of countless generations of inhabitants of this land, whose ways were marked by great respect for the natural resources of land and river, of forest and plain and desert" (§1). He noted that the encounter of early Native cultures with European culture "was a harsh and painful reality for your peoples. The cultural oppression, the injustices, the disruption of your life and of your traditional societies must be acknowledged" (§2). He also noted that there were positive aspects of the encounter, such as the work of missionaries who "strenuously defended the rights of the original inhabitants of this land," established missions, and proclaimed the gospel (§2). In an affirmation of Native cultures, he declared:

> I encourage you, as native people belonging to the different tribes and nations in the East, South, West and North, to preserve and keep alive your cultures, your languages, the values and customs which have served you well in the past and which provide a solid foundation for the future....We should all be grateful for the growing unity, presence, voice and leadership of Catholic native Americans in the church today. (§4)

He stated that there were social issues to be addressed to remedy the situation of Native peoples: "All consciences must be challenged. There are real injustices to be addressed, and biased attitudes to be changed" (§6).

Indigenous cultures were particularly affirmed in late July 2002, when the pope traveled to Central America and Mexico to canonize the first saints native to those places. In Guatemala on the occasion of the canonization of Central America's first saint, Brother Pedro de San José de Betancurt, he expressed his "appreciation and closeness to the many indigenous people," and declared, "Build the future responsibly, work for the harmonious progress of your peoples! You deserve all respect and have the right to fulfil yourselves completely, in justice, integral development and peace." [9] In Mexico City, at the Basilica of Our Lady of Guadalupe, located on what is believed to be the site of Mary's apparitions to the *indio* Juan Diego Cuauhtlatoatzin, the pope canonized this indigenous peasant. On this occasion, he thanked God for "the gift of the first indigenous Saint of the American

Continent," addressed "a very affectionate greeting to the many indigenous people who have come," urged the people of Mexico to "support the indigenous people in their legitimate aspirations, respecting and defending the authentic values of each ethnic group," and stated that Juan Diego accepted the Christian message "without foregoing his indigenous identity." [10]

John Paul's teachings at times transcended their anthropocentric foundation. He declared that people are responsible for creation, as images of God the Creator, and as such are to exercise conservative stewardship of the Earth entrusted to their care; and people have the right to work to gather from the bounty of the Earth those goods necessary to meet human needs. His developing environmental theology has been complemented by ideas presented in other addresses and documents with a Vatican base, including at the Earth Summit and in the *Catholic Catechism*.

Archbishop Renato Martino at the Earth Summit

At the United Nations Conference on the Environment and Development (UNCED, also known as the "Earth Summit") held in Rio de Janeiro, Brazil, in June 1992, Archbishop Renato R. Martino represented the Vatican as the Apostolic Nuncio and Head of the Delegation of the Holy See (the Vatican's designation as a nation-state in the United Nations). In his address to the gathered UN delegates, Archbishop Martino focused on what had become the twofold focus of Vatican environmental policy: ecological needs and economic needs. He stated that people are responsible both for creation as a whole and for a just distribution of the goods provided by creation. Martino noted that "the responsibility to respect all creation" complements respect for human life, and that the universe and the biotic community "are a testimony to God's creative power," God's love, and God's enduring presence.[11]

Martino linked concern for the environment with concern for the poor. He spoke of the obligations of stewardship and solidarity: stewardship for God's creation and "solidarity of universal dimensions, a 'cosmic fraternity' animated by the very love that flows from God." He stated that people must live in harmony with God, each other, and "with creation itself." (Martino departed here from the prior church position that the Earth and Earth's goods and creatures are intended by God for human appropriation and are dedicated to human use.)

Archbishop Martino also addressed the population issue, stating that contrary to people's misinterpretation of the church's position,

> the Catholic Church does not propose procreation at any cost....It is the right of the spouses to decide on the size of the family and spacing of births, without pressures from governments and organizations....What the Church opposes is the imposition of demographic policies and the promotion of methods for limiting births which are contrary to the objective moral order and to the liberty, dignity and conscience of the human being.[12]

Martino stated a Vatican policy that married couples have the right to decide on the number of children to have, but must use birth control methods congruent with an "objective moral order" and, by implication for Catholics, approved by the church.

In the late summer of 2002, at the "World Summit on Sustainable Development" (WSSD) hosted by the United Nations in Johannesburg, South Africa, on the tenth anniversary of the Rio Earth Summit, Archbishop Martino again headed the Holy See delegation. In his comments there, he urged an "ecological conversion" and concern for human dignity in considerations of sustainable development; called for "a profound change in modern civilization's patterns of consumption and production, particularly in the industrialized countries"; and pleaded for concrete action from the assembled delegates.[13]

The *Catechism of the Catholic Church:*
Creation and the Common Good

The *Catechism of the Catholic Church* (1994)[14] intermingled diverse attitudes toward environmental issues. Anthropocentrism was still very much in evidence, but again, it was a diffused anthropocentrism: that is, "man" was still at the top of a biotic hierarchy, but it was a collective "man." Additionally, the *Catechism* acknowledged that each creature has its particular goodness, which must be respected, and that creatures are interdependent. The sections on creation, the seventh commandment, and the common good articulated a human-centered focus and advocated a needs-based property distribution when discussing Earth and Earth's goods.

In the section "God creates an ordered and good world," for example, the *Catechism* declared that because creation emerges from God's goodness it is good also, and added that "God willed creation as a gift addressed to man, an inheritance destined for and entrusted to him" (§299). (The statement began by stating that creation was declared good by God, and has an *intrinsic* goodness, then called creation a "gift" for humanity, which implies an *instrumental* goodness.)

The *Catechism* stated that God is "present to his creatures' inmost being," citing Acts 17:28 (§300), and that creation has "its own goodness and proper perfection" but is not yet complete: it was "created 'in a state of journeying' *(in statu viae)* toward an ultimate perfection yet to be attained, to which God has destined it" (§302). Since each creature has its own goodness and perfection, humankind must respect this in every creature, lest there occur "disastrous consequences for human beings and their environment" (§339).

While affirming that "God wills the *interdependence* of creatures" (§340), the *Catechism* also stated that "God created everything for man, but man in turn was created to serve and love God and to offer all creation back to him" (§358), because God's plan is that "man and woman have the vocation of 'subduing' the earth as stewards of God," not with "an arbitrary and destructive domination," but, since they are "made in the image of the Creator 'who loves everything that exists,'" with "responsibility for the world God has entrusted to them" (§373).

There was a nod toward theories of evolution in these ideas, and an acknowledgment of the dynamic processes of the universe; an affirmation of the intrinsic goodness of all creatures (they are not good solely because they benefit humankind); and a recognition of the interdependence of living beings. A strong anthropocentrism (unintentionally bordering on idolatry) was expressed in the phrase, "God created everything for man," and was reinforced in the endorsement of the concept of humans "subduing" the Earth; this is diminished somewhat in the statement that people are to be "responsible." The *Catechism* also linked "images of the Creator" to love for "everything that exists" and to care for all creatures; but the latter idea also elevated humans, to some extent, to a divine plane, or at least to a hierarchical level above and over other creatures—not only in that humankind is made in God's image, but also in that people are responsible, from a superior position, for the world, a world that God has entrusted to *them*. Here again, there is a qualifier: "entrusted" replaces the phrase "given to them," which has been used often in Christian thought and is implied in the earlier mentioned phrase, "God created everything for man."

The goods of creation, according to the *Catechism* in its teachings on the seventh commandment,[15] are destined ultimately to benefit humanity. People are to use them wisely and well and to distribute them justly, including intergenerationally; and there should be respect for "the integrity of creation" (§2415).

Complementary ideas were expressed in the sections on the "common good" in the *Catechism,* which stated that "the good of each individual is necessarily related to the common good" (§1905), which means "'the sum total of social conditions which allow people, either as groups or as individuals, to reach their fulfillment more fully and more easily.' The common good concerns the life of all' [GS 26 §1; cf. GS 74 §1]" (§1906). This integration of the teachings on creation and on the common good provides a basis for further exploration both of the inherent goodness of creation and of how that goodness can benefit all members of the biotic community and Earth as a whole.

The developing environmental theology emerging from Rome in the latter decades of the twentieth century and into the new millennium carried forth ideas first explored at Vatican II and developed several of them further. Concepts of human hierarchy in creation were generally retained; new insights about a Christian responsibility to be caring in creation were added; and the rights of all people to share ownership of Earth's land and the use of Earth's goods were reinforced.

As bishops across the globe considered issues of economic injustice and environmental degradation, they issued pastoral letters from their particular national contexts. These statements built upon biblical and Vatican traditions, but incorporated additional insights from theologians and environmental writers and organizations. The adaptation of traditional thought to local ecological and social conditions in these pastoral documents began a transformation—not only of the national social contexts in which they were released, but also of the Catholic environmental theological tradition itself.

2
Common Ground
and Common Good

The seeds of environmental theology planted by Vatican-based documents stimulated and were complemented by pastoral statements issued by national conferences of bishops. Among these were letters released by the bishops of the Dominican Republic, Guatemala, and the United States. The Latin American documents preceded the release of Pope John Paul II's *Ecological Crisis* message, and provide few insights into the care of creation in itself, focusing instead on church teachings about land ownership and distribution of Earth's goods. The North American statements followed the pope's message, and included both the traditional focus of the letters from the South and innovative understandings on the role of people in creation and their relation to creation.

The Dominican Episcopal Conference: *Pastoral Letter on the Relationship of Human Beings to Nature*

In 1987, the bishops of the Dominican Republic expressed in a pastoral letter[1] their concerns about the deteriorating environment and oppressive social conditions in their island nation. The document was heavily permeated with anthropocentric attitudes, although sometimes the anthropocentrism was modified. The bishops stated that everyone has a moral obligation to maintain and defend "the necessary ecological balance" and that "to abuse natural resources" is "to act against nature" (§50). They also called on Catholic colleges and schools "to include instruction on ecology from the very first years" and to instill in future generations "a profound love and respect for nature," making them aware that "morality extends also to this" (§82). Overall, the letter called for increased human responsibility for Nature and the elimination of political corruption, greed, and conditions of extreme poverty that contribute to the deteriorating environment. Particular areas of ecological focus noted were deforestation and waterways devastation.

The bishops opened their letter by recalling a 1982 pastoral letter in which they had declared that "the sin of humanity against nature always has its repercussions against humanity itself" (§1). Two key ideas were thereby presented: Human acts that harm Nature are *sins;* and human self-interest is harmed as a consequence. The designation "sin" brought in moral considerations and moral condemnation; the appeal to self-interest, while not the ideal approach to exhort people to change their ways, was perhaps seen to be the most practical political and economic approach for obtaining concrete results from a moral exhortation. The self-interest appeal was evident also in the bishops' approving citation of Pope Paul VI's statement (from *Octogesima Adveniens* §21) that through "an irrational and inattentive exploitation of nature, man can destroy it and become a victim of his own depravity" (§19). The bishops also spoke of "concrete crimes against nature" (§4), reinforcing the use of a moral judgment, "sin," with the use of a legal designation, "crime." The essential message of the letter was encapsulated in its quote (§2) from Pope John Paul's *Redemptor Hominis* (1979): "It was the Creator's will that man should communicate with nature as an intelligent and noble 'master' and 'guardian,' and not as a heedless 'exploiter' and 'destroyer.'"

The Dominican bishops affirmed throughout their statement humankind's position over Earth, over Earth's other creatures, and over creation as a whole: God had put human beings "in charge over the earth" (§31), and to humanity as a whole "gave as *common patrimony* the earth and all that it contains" (§32). Humans improve the Earth, because "God gave humankind the task and the obligation to 'rule and govern' the earth through science and technology and in this way to make it ever more useful for the perfection of human beings and of society" (§33). The latter statement, which might out of context be used to justify technologically based ecological destruction, was immediately qualified in a way that limits irresponsible uses of science and technology and also affirms God's ultimate sovereignty over creation: "To use human intelligence and skills (science and technology) to destroy or to threaten the earth, or not to use them when difficulties or new and varied challenges arise, is a contradiction, an abuse of the divine plan, and an affront to the will of the Creator who is absolute Lord of the earth and of humankind" (§34).

The bishops' view of humans' superior position in Nature went beyond their view that Nature is to serve humanity. They stated that "nature *depends* on human beings who...must preserve, defend, *better,* and *perfect it*" (§17; italics added); and humans have serious obligations to Nature, "which *depends* on us" (§36). Scientists would take issue with the idea that Nature "depends on" human beings; many theologians would question whether people are called to make God's creation "better" or to "perfect it," or that this perfecting is done by humans as *administrators* of creation: "The ongoing perfection of human nature includes the growing perfection of the natural environment of which human beings are, as we have said, custodians and faithful and intelligent administrators" (§55).

Again, it should be noted that human dominion is not to be entirely self-serving, in the sense of satisfying individual or social class or commercial greed, but in the interests of the human community, with a particular concern for the poor. The latter at times use environmentally harmful practices from necessity: rural people's misery drives them to marginal lands "with no other option than to make intensive use of the land" (§23); the "poorest in the country" use "slash and burn" techniques just to survive and to "eke out a precarious living" (§24).

The bishops took to task the exploitation of the nonrenewable resources of their country by foreign nations and corporations: "The highly industrialized and developed countries may not exercise a sort of monopoly on the exploitation and use of these resources" (§42).

The letter briefly mentioned population issues, noting that there is "an accelerated population growth accompanied by an ever-increasing demand for food, resources, and energy" (§20). As in other church documents, intergenerational responsibility toward human descendants was a concern: ecological devastation "threatens the possibility of the life of future generations" (§16); people must pass the Earth on "to those who come after us, not in a deteriorated condition but in an improved state" (§35); the ongoing use of natural resources should be "taking into consideration the needs of the whole human family both present and future" (§37).

The bishops offered several action suggestions (§58–§82), and noted that Saint Francis of Assisi should be a model for people to emulate to reconcile humans among themselves, and "between them and all of nature" (§56).

The Dominican Republic pastoral letter, then, strongly called on people of the island of all social classes and occupations to act more responsibly to care for Earth's goods on their national territory. This call was phrased in anthropocentric tones, but the anthropocentrism was tempered to a degree by suggestions of distributive justice practices and by love for Nature, and by placing anthropocentrism in a context of subordination to God's ultimate sovereignty. The document contributed to environmental theology by calling ecological devastation a "sin," and by noting that while rich and poor people both harm their environment, the poor

do so out of their desperation to survive, and so the social conditions that provoke this should be changed.

The Guatemalan Bishops' Conference: *The Cry for Land*

The bishops of Guatemala, concerned particularly about the
plight of the landless poor, issued their pastoral letter, *The Cry for
Land,* in 1988. While the letter[2] does not specifically address
environmental degradation, it does emphasize other aspects of
Catholic teachings about human responsibilities in creation: that
property in land and the goods of Earth be equitably distributed,
and that people receive just compensation for the work they do
with materials taken from Earth's bounty.

The bishops opened their letter with an extraordinary
insight: that the cry for land is the "most desperate cry heard in
Guatemala," a cry that "bursts forth from millions of Guatemalan
hearts yearning not only to possess the land, but to be possessed
by it" (§0.1). The paragraph began with an acknowledgment that
landless people need land for life and livelihood, then added the
idea that when they have the land not only will they possess it,
they will be "possessed by it." Here is a consciousness that people
must respect and nurture and work with Earth not as mere property but as an entity that is engaged with those who work it. The
idea was not developed later in the letter, but it did provide a
foundation for the development of an environmental awareness,
even while the primary focus of the bishops' thought then was on
land redistribution. The opening paragraph also had a passing reference to indigenous peoples' right to land, stating that the
"People of Corn" are like "strangers in the land which belonged
to them for thousands of years," and are "considered second-class
citizens in the nation forged by their extraordinary ancestors."

The bishops stated that "the breach between classes continues to widen, even amidst a people who profess to be Christian"
(§1.1.1), suggesting both that the widening gap is immoral and
that Christians should not approve of the conditions in which the

poor are forced to live. They declared that impoverished rural people are enduring a "calvary of suffering," a result of their "dispossession of the land" (§1.1.3.1); by contrast, "the majority of the arable land is in the hands of a privileged few" (§1.1.3.2).

Use of land for food production for domestic consumption is subordinated to use of land for export purposes, since the "agricultural export sector, owning huge and fertile land areas, holds the best arable lands and the means of agricultural production" (§1.4.1.1). The few *campesinos* (agricultural workers) who own land make do with less productive land, and to eke out a living or provide food for themselves they use practices "which are very damaging to the ecology" (§1.4.1.2). Marginalized *campesinos* are kept in their places by "the very structure of Guatemalan society which is organized for the benefit of a minority and with no regard for the vast majority of Guatemalans" (§1.4.2.2). As a consequence, "the campesino is frequently exploited in a ruthless and inhumane way" (§1.4.3.1), and "violence in the rural area is common" (§1.4.5.1).

In their theological reflections, the bishops offered a very anthropocentric view of the human role on Earth, but forcefully advocated just wages for workers and a place for them on the land. They stated that the theological basis for human dignity derives from people being made in the "image of God," and declared that "the earth is, then, according to God's plan, humanity's world" (§2.1.1); the latter was later qualified: "The earth does not belong to men but to the Lord, and what each one calls his property is in reality the portion to which he is entitled in order to make a living. The earth is the Lord's and the bounty thereof, the world and those who inhabit therein (Ps 24:1)" (§2.1.3).

The bishops declared that "liberation begins for creation when the goods of the earth cease to be instruments of human rivalry and exploitation in order to become a means of friendship and communion" (§2.1.6), and observed that faith in Christ risen "and the friendship which thus results lead to a new earth in which justice is at home (2 Pt 3:13)"; until that time comes, people "may make of this earth a place of togetherness in justice and equity" (§2.1.7).

The bishops stated that there is a "social purpose to property" and quoted the statement of Pope John Paul II at the Third General Conference of Latin American Bishops that "'upon all private property there is a grave *social responsibility*' (literally, a social *mortgage*)"; from this it follows that "the right to private property is not an absolute right, but rather a conditional one," since God intends a universal destination for the goods of the Earth (§2.2.1). They elaborated on this by citing early church documents and declaring that "community of goods is therefore a form of existence more adequate to our nature than is private property itself" (§2.2.2).

In their pastoral conclusions, the Guatemalan bishops declared that "the campesinos' cry has been stifled by the power of arms. Thousands of campesinos have been killed in Guatemala merely for having attempted a change of structure" (§3.1.4). The bishops called for a change from the "sinful structures" in their country (§3.2.1; §3.2.4.1); a *solidarity* that is "the opposite of egotistical individualism" (§3.2.2.1); "authentic human and social development" that includes economic development (§3.2.3.1); and an "equitable land distribution" (§3.2.4.3), among other things, all of which should be accomplished through nonviolence (§3.2.5.1). There was no elaboration on how nonviolence would work; the tactic of land occupations by landless *campesinos* is not to be used (§3.2.5.2); the bishops hoped that "personal conversion" would be effective (§4.3). They stated that their role was not to suggest solutions: "Our pastoral service is limited to a posing of the problem" (§4.4).

The bishops of Guatemala, then, analyzed injustices related to land ownership and use in terms of how those injustices impact human communities, particularly the rural poor. Except for their intriguing statement about rural people being "possessed by" the land, they did not address environmental degradation or human responsibility to care for creation, and while speaking against land occupation and armed revolution, they proposed no concrete alternative action to alter the oppression suffered by rural people.

The U.S. Bishops: *Renewing the Earth*

In their 1991 document, *Renewing the Earth: An Invitation to Reflection and Action in Light of Catholic Social Teaching,*[3] the U.S. bishops declared that "at its core the environmental crisis is a moral challenge. It calls us to examine how we use and share the goods of the earth, what we pass on to future generations and how we live in harmony with God's creation."[4] After noting aspects of the degradation of the environment, the bishops stated that "we must seek a society where economic life and environmental commitment work together to protect and enhance life on this planet."[5] Relating the needs of people and planet, the bishops declared that they "seek to explore the links between concern for the person and for the earth, between natural ecology and social ecology. The web of life is one...."[6]

The bishops noted the relationship between poverty and environmental degradation, stating that "it is the poor and powerless who most directly bear the burden of current environmental carelessness."[7]

The bishops linked natural ecology and social ecology when they posed questions about the relationship between "justice and duties to the environment," about confronting "possible conflicts between environment and jobs," and about how they might seek the common good and develop ways to "value both people and the earth."[8]

The document called people to conversion, and to care for the Earth while being aware of their intergenerational responsibility: "We need a change of heart to preserve and protect the planet for our children and for generations yet unborn."[9] The bishops noted that people are related to creation, and as part of the natural world they must care for their earthly home.[10]

The bishops affirmed, here and elsewhere in their letter, that "the fundamental relation between humanity and nature is one of caring for creation."[11]

Renewing the Earth has made a major contribution to Catholic environmental thought through its discussion of a "sacramental universe." The bishops wrote:

> Throughout history, people have continued to meet the Creator on mountaintops, in vast deserts, and alongside waterfalls and gently flowing springs. In storms and earthquakes, they found expressions of divine power. In the cycle of the seasons and the courses of the stars, they have discerned signs of God's fidelity and wisdom. We still share, though dimly, in that sense of God's presence in nature.[12]
>
> For many people, the environmental movement has reawakened appreciation of the truth that, through the created gifts of nature, men and women encounter their Creator. The Christian vision of a sacramental universe — a world that discloses the Creator's presence by visible and tangible signs — can contribute to making the earth a home for the human family once again.[13]

The sacramental sense of Nature could promote stewardship of creation, the bishops observed, because people conscious of and reverencing God's presence in creation would see themselves as part of creation, and care for it.[14]

The universe is God's dwelling and creation. In it, people can encounter God through the created goods of the natural world. The idea of a "sacramental universe" gives a contemporary expression to the teaching from Wisdom that exclaims, "From the greatness and the beauty of created things their original author, by analogy, is seen" (13:5). People can see the hand and plan of the Creator in creation. Therefore, "it is appropriate that we treat other creatures and the natural world not just as means to human fulfillment, but as God's creatures, possessing an independent value, worthy of our respect and care."[15] The teaching here contradicts the perspective of those who believe that other creatures only have worth to the extent that they serve human needs and wants, a perspective evident, as noted, in some earlier church documents.

The bishops called for solidarity, which "requires sacrifices of our own self-interest for the good of others and of the earth we share."[16] Humanity should move toward "an environmentally sustainable economy" that has "a just economic system which equitably shares the bounty of the earth and of human enterprise with all peoples."[17] The latter means that there will be justice for the poor and jobs for workers: employment and environment cannot be exclusive concerns but must be considered jointly to benefit both Earth and workers, since "both impoverished peoples and an imperiled planet demand our committed service" and "Christian love forbids choosing between people and the planet."[18]

When discussing population issues, the bishops first noted a major problem with consumerism in the developed world, and then stated that "it must be acknowledged that rapid population growth presents special problems and challenges that must be addressed in order to avoid damage done to the environment and to social development."[19] The bishops noted that "at the very minimum we need food and energy policies that are socially just, environmentally benign and economically efficient,"[20] and concluded that "a just and sustainable society and world are not an optional ideal, but a moral and practical necessity. Without justice, a sustainable economy will be beyond reach. Without an ecologically responsible world economy, justice will be unachievable."[21]

The bishops would return to several of the themes of *Renewing the Earth* in their 1999 statement, *Sharing Catholic Social Teaching: Challenges and Directions.*[22] Among the social teachings the bishops emphasized there are those concerning humankind's responsibility to creation:

> On a planet conflicted over environmental issues, the Catholic tradition insists that we show our respect for the

Creator by our stewardship of creation. Care for the earth is
not just an Earth Day slogan; it is a requirement of our faith.
We are called to protect people and the planet, living our
faith in relation with all of God's creation.[23]

The phrase "a requirement of our faith" recalls John Paul II's
statement that care for creation is an "essential part" of Christian
faith (see p. 13).

The U.S. Bishops' Quincentenary Statement:
1992: A Time for Reconciling and Recommitting Ourselves as a People

In November 1991 the bishops issued a complementary
statement, *1992: A Time for Reconciling and Recommitting Ourselves as a People—Pastoral Reflections on the V Centenary and
Native American People*.[24] This letter carried forth ideas expressed
in a document issued twenty-five years earlier, *Statement of U.S.
Catholic Bishops on American Indians*.[25] In the earlier statement,
the bishops had declared that early missionaries had dedicated
themselves to promoting Christianity, but that while they so
labored the church sometimes failed to respect indigenous cultures. They noted that "faith finds expression in and through the
particular values, customs and institutions of the people who hear
it" (§8), and that "American Indian peoples had developed rich
and diverse cultures long before the first Europeans came to the
American continent" (§12). Over the years, Indians "have been
deprived of their communal lands" and lost "the traditional ves-
tiges of their culture" (§16). In the light of deprivations suffered by
Indians, the bishops declared that they had a "responsibility to join
with our American Indian sisters and brothers in their ongoing
struggle to secure justice" (§20). The bishops also acknowledged
their responsibility to examine, in light of the gospel and Catholic
social teachings, government policies and programs affecting
American Indians, and to urge that they be more just in such areas
as "the speedy and equitable resolution of treaty and statute

questions; protection of Indian land and resource rights"; and "increased levels of funding and technical assistance necessary to aid American Indians in achieving political and economic self-determination and full employment" (§25).

The quincentenary statement incorporated ideas from the earlier document, and recognized an important aspect of Indian/Native American[26] traditions: the relationship between Earth and Native spirituality (implicitly recognizing that Native religions embody much of the respect for creation proclaimed by Catholic Church leaders in other documents cited). The bishops acknowledged the importance of Native traditions in their statement and apologized for the harsh treatment of Native peoples in the past, including by misguided missionaries. Then they indicated, in a significant statement presenting an attitude not present in earlier eras of church-Indian engagement: "The coming of religious faith in this land began not 500 years ago, but centuries before in the prayers, chants, dance and other sacred celebrations of Native people."[27] This brief statement recognized the spirituality of Indian peoples in a very direct way and negated prior missionaries' assertions that Indians did not worship God; the statement suggests (perhaps unconsciously) that different cultures might worship the same Spirit in different ways and under different names.

The bishops called for remembering Native peoples' sufferings from the past; reconciliation between Native and Euro-Americans, "a genuine reconciliation between the essential traditions of Catholic faith and the best of the traditions of Native American life, each respecting, shaping and enriching the other";[28] and recommitment on the part of the church to Native Americans, "to stand with native peoples in their search for greater justice in our society."[29] Regarding treaty rights, the bishops declared that they renew their commitment "to press for justice in the prompt and fair adjudication of treaty rights....Native Americans have the right to be self-determining, to decide the ways their land and natural resources on those lands are used for the benefit of their people and for the broader common good."[30]

The statements about American Indian peoples indicated a heightened respect, on the part of church leaders, for non-Christian and non-Western cultures and spirituality. The recognition of traditional indigenous faith, in particular, marked a profound shift from earlier Christian missionary attitudes toward and practices in indigenous communities of the Americas.

The U.S. Bishops: *Global Climate Change: A Plea for Dialogue, Prudence and the Common Good*

The bishops of the United States issued their *Global Climate Change* environmental pastoral letter in 2001, the tenth anniversary of *Renewing the Earth*. In it, they addressed the issue cited in the title and issues related to it, and offered moral and theological reflections on them.

In the first sentence of the Introduction, the bishops cited Psalm 24:1, which declares that "the earth is the Lord's and all it holds," and immediately stated that the Creator gave humans the "gift" of creation.[31] The statement throughout wove back and forth between the somewhat contradictory concepts of "gift" and "stewardship," the former implying that God has given over creation and its constituent parts to humanity, and the latter insisting that humanity care for what is God's, a creation that God has entrusted to humanity. (The giver parts with a gift, and the recipient may do as they choose with what is given to them; a trust, by contrast, is retained by the one who assigns its safekeeping to another: "stewardship" is the exercise of responsibility for a "trust.") The idea that creation is a "gift" seems to take precedence over stewardship. Although stewardship is described at length midway through the letter,[32] "gift" is the major theme of the Conclusion of the letter, being mentioned there four times.[33] In any case, a clear message does emerge: People are to use wisely the goods of creation. In the matter at hand, this means that the way humans respond "to global climate change should be a sign of our respect for God's creation." The first paragraph also noted that God found all creation "very good."

Throughout the document, the bishops chastised the abuse of science to meet partisan or pecuniary interests. They lamented that in the discussion of global climate change, "the search for the common good and the voices of poor people and poor countries sometimes are neglected,"[34] and so they take up the cause of the poor, noting that "the common good requires solidarity with the poor."[35] Paralleling the Dominican bishops' letter's statement that some environmental degradation is caused by the poor because of their need, the U.S. bishops observed that "many of the poor in these [developing] countries live in degrading and desperate situations that often lead them to adopt environmentally harmful agricultural and industrial practices."[36]

The pastoral suggested two basic moral questions that should be asked when people reflect on global climate change: How might people be "stewards of creation" in an era when they can alter creation in significant and even irrevocable ways? And, How might the family of nations be stewards by protecting creation and providing for the common good and justice-based economic and social progress?[37]

Population issues received more attention in this letter than in most other church letters. The bishops for the most part avoided taking on the issue directly, declaring instead that "voracious consumerism" in the industrialized countries is a major cause of environmental harm, and that the reduction of poverty "improved education and social conditions for women." They stated that "natural family planning and the education of women and men" would be "a more responsible approach to population issues."[38]

The bishops declared that responses to climate change should be guided by four moral values: "the universal common good, respect for God's creation, an option for the poor, and a sense of intergenerational obligation."[39] Intergenerational responsibility was advocated throughout the letter, as was a consciousness that the climate is "a part of the planetary commons."[40] The notion of a "commons" is not explored beyond this brief reference.

Suggestions for change included bearing in mind that private property has a "social mortgage," conserving energy, searching for new energy alternatives, and providing financial and technical assistance from the developed countries to the poorer developing countries.

The bishops' letter recognized that human activity is harming the global climate, cautioned against simplifying the data to justify one side or another in the debate over the extent to which this is the case, and called for measures to ameliorate a deteriorating situation. The bishops recommended prudence: while the evidence does not suggest that great harms are being done by human actions, this might be the case, and people should act with caution as a result.[41]

Global Climate Change brought to bear some of the major ideas that the national bishops had developed in *Renewing the Earth,* such as promotion of the common good, private property rights and responsibilities, and concern for the poor. However, the important teaching that the universe is "sacramental," an idea presented in the 1991 statement, was not mentioned in the 2001 letter.

In the national documents reviewed in this chapter, care for creation and concern for the common good, including compassion for the poor, are significant themes. In different historical situations and different historical moments, the emphasis is more on one than the other. But these basic teachings remain paramount in Catholic environmental theology, and are foundational in regional church documents.

3
Sacramental and Communal Creation

In North America, three decades of environmental consciousness in the broader culture stimulated complementary theological consideration of the role that the Christian religion has played and might play in relation to ecological issues. Catholic bishops in different regions of the United States and Canada began to analyze land issues in their particular social and ecological settings and to offer moral principles and exhortations for practical projects to alleviate harms to creation and to the human community. The goodness of creation was related to the common good in these pastoral letters, either explicitly or implicitly. These regional letters gave universal principles a regional locus, suggesting a sense of place for their implementation.

Appalachia, United States, 1975: *This Land Is Home to Me*

The Catholic bishops of Appalachia have been concerned about the extraordinary poverty of their region, particularly vis-à-vis the mineral wealth extracted from it, especially by coal companies. On February 1, 1975, twenty-six bishops of the region issued *This Land Is Home to Me — A Pastoral Letter on Powerlessness in Appalachia.*[1]

The letter, written in a conversational, free-verse poetic style, stated very forcefully the connection between powerlessness and poverty in Appalachia. The bishops noted that the "people who live in the hills, who love nature's freedom and beauty, who are alive with song and poetry" are also "poor and suffer oppression." To their struggle in the mountains for justice, there are added "struggles in industrial centers, grown grey with smoke and smog," and "struggle in farmland...where little farmers and sharecroppers" battle for food, dignity, and security. All of these groups in struggle are tied together "by the mountain chain and by the coal" that is central to the region.[2] In powerful words, the bishops declared:

> There is a saying in the region
> that coal is king.
> That's not exactly right.
> The kings are those who control big coal,
> and the profit and power
> which comes from it.
> Many of these kings
> don't live in the region.[3]

In these brief lines the bishops alluded to issues surrounding the use of wealth produced by coal: this wealth is appropriated by a minority of people who own the coal companies and profit greatly from them; and this minority exercises absentee ownership of an industry that has devastating impacts on the ecological and economic health of the region and of its poor majority. After discussing the close of some coal operations and the plight of workers who migrate to cities to look for jobs but often find none, the bishops noted that "it is a strange system which makes people suffer both when they have work and when they don't have work."[4] The bishops observed that "corporate giants" create a way of life whose "forces become perverted, hostile to the dignity of the earth and of its people."[5] The bishops here expressed concern for the environment as well as for the people who inhabit it, noting that both people and environment have a dignity that should be respected. The bishops went on to lament that "a country which took such richness from Appalachia left so little for the people. Great fortunes were built on the exploitation of Appalachian workers and Appalachian resources...."[6] Here again, the theme of concern for the common good was expressed in regional terms, linked to devastation of Appalachia's land. In response to those who might assert about the situation that "that's economics," the bishops responded that "economics is made by people. Its principles don't fall down from the sky and remain for all eternity."[7]

In the next part of the letter, the bishops declared that "the living God, the Lord whom we worship, is the God of the poor"[8] and added, "The church continues, despite its sins, working for the poor, insisting on practical love, and not just prayers and good intentions"; when the church strays from its task to work for justice, "the Spirit is alive within it, stirring up new voices to call it back to its mission for justice."[9] The bishops later stated that "a new social order is being born," and that the goal of the struggle for justice is "citizen control, or community control. The people themselves must shape their own destiny."[10] In their Conclusion, the Appalachian bishops urged people "to be a part of the rebirth of utopias," to listen to the voice of the Lord inspiring their dream of justice.[11]

Heartland America, 1980: *Strangers and Guests*

The next regional bishops' pastoral letter was issued five years later, in the U.S. Midwest, after Catholic farmers suggested to their bishops that they should issue a region-appropriate letter that paralleled the Appalachian document. The result was *Strangers and Guests: Toward Community in the Heartland,*[12] issued on May 1, 1980, by all of the seventy-two active and retired bishops of a twelve-state area.

In *Strangers and Guests,* the bishops noted that "the earth all too frequently is being subjected to harmful farming, mining and development practices" (§1). People's opportunity to live "a productive and rewarding life" is determined largely by their relationship to the land, which should be a relationship of "cooperative harmony, for the land—complemented in nature by water and air—is our most important and limited natural resource." This "resource" should be conserved with its goods and beauty "to benefit present and future generations at home and abroad" (§7). The bishops expressed their hope for "the social reforms that are necessary to preserve our land and the best of our heritage, and promote justice for our people" (§8).

There was a strong focus in *Strangers and Guests* on protecting and promoting the owner-operated family farm, as might be expected from a midwestern bishops' land pastoral. But the letter also addressed issues of mining, forestry, chemical pollution, housing for the poor, transportation, and energy use. As a theological basis for care for God's creation, the bishops offered ten "Principles of Land Stewardship":

1. The land is God's.
2. People are God's stewards on the land.
3. The land's benefits are for everyone.
4. The land should be distributed equitably.
5. The land should be conserved and restored.
6. Land use planning must consider social and environmental impacts.
7. Land use should be appropriate to land quality.
8. The land should provide a moderate livelihood.
9. The land's workers should be able to become the land's owners.
10. The land's mineral wealth should be shared. (§50)

In these principles, important seeds were planted for an integral land ethic. The bishops elaborated: God has "ultimate dominion" of the Earth (§51); the Earth is "entrusted to humanity's care" (§52); people are God's stewards (§53–54) and are "co-creators with God in guiding the land's productive power and in conserving the land's natural gifts. As co-creators, God's stewards help the land fulfill the purpose for which God created it: to help satisfy the physical, social and spiritual needs of God's creatures" (§55). Thus all of "God's creatures," not just humans, are God's concern. Here the pastoral letter negated the anthropocentrism, common to several church statements, that sees the Earth and its goods as created by God ultimately or even solely to satisfy human needs.

The midwestern bishops advocated equitable distribution of Earth's goods in the human community; proposed widespread land ownership in the human community, including through distribution by means of a progressive land tax (§89); and supported struggles for justice of Native Americans (§103).

In support of the bishops and in affirmation of rural life, Pope John Paul II visited the Diocese of Des Moines, Iowa, in early October 1979. In his homily at Living History Farms on October 4, his message addressed to farmers emphasized stewardship of God's creation:

> The land is God's gift entrusted to humanity from the very beginning.…The land is not only God's gift, it is also man's responsibility.…The land must be conserved with care since it is intended to be fruitful for generation upon generation.…You are stewards of some of the most important resources that God has entrusted to humanity. Therefore, conserve the land well, so that your children's children and generations after them will inherit an even richer land than was entrusted to you.[13]

John Paul here suggested several elements of an ongoing land ethic: land as a *trust* (which is more fundamental and demanding than a "gift," since it is ultimately held on behalf of another); human *responsibility* to care for the land; *intergenerational responsibility* on the part of those who own or manage the land; *conservation* of the land and its goods; and an implied *cooperation* with God, a participation with God's creative action and Earth's rhythms so that Earth might become ever more fruitful. There still lingered, however, the perception that Earth and its goods ultimately are intended only to benefit humanity, a perception that would be altered just over a decade later, as seen earlier, in John Paul's 1990 message, *The Ecological Crisis: A Common Responsibility.*

Northwestern United States, 1987: "A Public Declaration: To the Tribal Councils and Traditional Spiritual Leaders of the Indian and Eskimo Peoples of the Pacific Northwest"

In November 1987, bishops and regional leaders from nine Christian denominations, including Archbishop Raymond Hunthausen and Bishop Thomas Murphy from the Seattle Archdiocese, issued a "Public Declaration"[14] about the relationship of their respective churches with Native peoples in the Northwest. The letter began with "a formal apology on behalf of our churches for their long-standing participation in the destruction of traditional Native American spiritual practices," and acknowledged that the churches "have frequently been unconscious and insensitive and have not come to your aid when you have been victimized by Federal policies and practices." The church leaders asked the members of their churches to recognize and respect "traditional ways of life" and to protect "sacred places and ceremonial objects."

The statement affirmed the rights of Native peoples to hold "traditional ceremonies and rituals," to have "access to and protection of sacred sites" and use of public lands for their ceremonies, and to be able to use customary religious symbols and objects in their worship.

The Christian leaders declared that the "spiritual power of the land and the ancient wisdom of your indigenous religions can be, we believe, great gifts to the Christian churches," and

committed themselves to aid in "righting previous wrongs."
They concluded with a prayer: "May the God of Abraham and
Sarah, and the Spirit who lives in both the cedar and Salmon
People be honored and celebrated."

The declaration is significant in that it offers an apology for
past wrongs committed against Native peoples by the churches,
acknowledges that the churches can learn from Native spiritual
traditions, and pledges the churches' support in safeguarding this
spiritual heritage. As did the U.S. bishops' 1992 quincentenary
letter, the declaration affirms the spirituality of Native peoples, in
contrast to earlier missionaries' perspectives and efforts to eliminate it. It is a distinctive ecumenical document in two ways: the
unity of the church leaders issuing the declaration; and the extension of that unity of faith in the Spirit to traditional Native spiritual leaders.

Appalachia, United States, 1995: *At Home in the Web of Life*

The bishops of Appalachia issued *At Home in the Web of
Life*[15] to commemorate the twentieth anniversary of *This Land Is
Home to Me*. Written in poetic free verse, as was its predecessor
Appalachian document, it focused on sustainable communities
and a sustainable environment for the region.

The bishops defined *sustainable communities* as "communities where people and the rest of nature can live together in harmony and not rob future generations,"[16] and declared that people
are "called to form sustainable communities, and to develop sustainable livelihoods, all in sacred creative communion with land
and forest and water and air, indeed with all Earth's holy creatures."[17] A sense of kinship with and respect for all members of
both the biotic and abiotic communities is presented: there is to be
"creative communion" among people and other members of creation, who are "holy creatures." The bishops later placed these
creatures within a great outdoor cathedral: "In this magnificent
work of God's creation, misty mountain haze is holy incense, tall

tree trunks are temple pillars, sun-splashed leaves are stained glass, and song-birds are angelic choirs."[18]

The bishops linked environmental degradation with economic deprivation, declaring, "We do not see the crisis of nature as separate from the crisis of the poor, but see both as a single crisis of community."[19]

The letter poetically described a sense of awe before a creation that reveals "the loving face of the Creator,"[20] and called people, as God's images, "to care in love for our precious Earth, as if Earth were God's own garden, just as God cares in love for all creation."[21] When people act in creation with humility, they are faithful "children of our mother Earth. With her we are all creatures of the one Creator and Redeemer."[22]

The pastoral also reflected on property relationships and their relationship to justice, from a perspective of creation being not a gift but a trust from God. Private property must serve the community, for "no one truly owns any part of creation. Rather all creation belongs only to God." People might be responsible to care for parts of it, as long as they serve others' needs as well as they serve their own.[23] The time has come for "just and legal land reform."[24] Property is "for the common good," and most property "should be rooted in the local community."[25]

The bishops called for a "return to the traditional Catholic teaching about the common good," but extended the concept of "common good" beyond the human family to "the common good of all people, the common good of the entire ecosystem, the common good of the whole web of life."[26] With these words, this Appalachian letter contained the seeds for the growth of a *relational consciousness* and commitment to the well-being of all creation, an alternative to and a step beyond the dominion and stewardship perspectives expressed in other church documents.

New Mexico, 1998:
Reclaiming the Vocation to Care for the Earth

In their environmental pastoral letter,[27] the bishops of New Mexico noted global and regional forms of environmental devastation, then focused on issues in their state: protection and equitable use of water; waste deposits; and mining pollution. Turning to scripture, they commented upon Genesis 1:26, noting first that humankind was created to "'have dominion' over all creation," but immediately stated that "the use of *dominion* in Genesis does not imply unrestrained exploitation; rather it is a term describing a 'representative' and how that person is to behave on behalf of the one who sends the representative. We are God's representatives. Therefore we are to treat nature as the Creator would, not for our own selfish consumption but for the good of all creation."

This means, according to the bishops, that people are "to reclaim our vocation as responsible caretakers of the earth, its living and natural resources"; and "to continue the creative work of God, enhancing this place we call home," which includes "ensuring that nature continues to thrive as God intended."

The bishops affirmed the sacramental nature of creation: "Catholic tradition has consistently seen the universe as God's dwelling and therefore affirms a sacramental dimension to it." The bishops reiterated this teaching when they listed, as a theme in Catholic social justice, "a God-centered and sacramental view of the universe, which grounds human accountability for the fate of the earth." Other themes included global interdependence, the common good, an equitable use of the Earth's resources, an option for the poor, and "limits of material growth."[28]

The bishops called for several action steps, including "the conversion of our hearts and minds," "reclaiming our vocation as God's stewards of all creation," and teaching environmental ethics in parishes. They urged public officials "to seek the common good, which includes the good of our planetary home, to eradicate actions and policies which perpetuate various forms of environmental racism and to work for an economy which focuses more on equitable sustainability," rather than on an "unbridled consumption of natural resources and acquisition of goods."[29]

The New Mexico pastoral letter is the only bishops' environmental statement that specifically mentions environmental racism. It recalled the "sacramental universe" theme first presented in *Renewing the Earth*. It qualified "dominion," and offered a "stewardship" understanding of the human role in creation. It advocated the common good and the exercise of an "option for the poor." This brief document encapsulated major teachings, and carried forth the new ideas of the sacramentality of creation and the justice-oriented "option for the poor."

Alberta, Canada, 1998: *Celebrate Life: Care for Creation*

Bishops in the Canadian province of Alberta issued *Celebrate Life: Care for Creation*[30] to reflect on regional environmental issues. They used the term "dominion over the earth" to refer to the human role in creation, but clarified it as "a dominion of service, wisdom and love."[31] At the same time, they acknowledged that "we need to affirm our place within the dynamic web of creation which supports and sustains all life."[32] All creation is integrated and evolving, and people must find their proper place in its web.

In a now-recurring theme in North American Catholic teachings, the bishops declared that "we can learn much from the spiritual traditions of our aboriginal brothers and sisters which celebrate our kinship with the rest of creation and seek to strengthen the sacred circle of all creation."[33]

Complementing comments by the U.S. bishops in *Renewing the Earth,* the Alberta bishops stated that "Catholics see creation in a 'sacramental' way....God is present and speaks in the dynamic life forces of our universe and planet as well as in our own lives. Respect for life needs to include all creation."[34] Harmful human conduct can affect sacramentality: "Ecological destruction and the loss of biodiversity obscure our ability to see and experience God and are an affront to the Creator."[35]

The bishops extended the idea of the "common good" beyond human communities, from meaning "the whole society being organized through its social, political and economic institutions so that all individuals, families and communities can thrive and seek their own good," to include "a healthy natural environment."[36] The theme of the "common good" was woven through statements about relationships within human communities, including in teachings about issues of poverty, population, and profits. There should be a special concern for "the poor and marginalized" in development programs.[37] Private property and accumulated wealth "are not an absolute right because these carry a 'social mortgage' at the service of the global common good."[38] The current economic model of "maximizing profit in an increasingly global market is unsustainable."[39]

Population issues were briefly addressed. The bishops stated that a "world of increasing population and widening inequality within nations and between nations…is already approaching real ecological limits….The earth can provide for everyone's needs, but not for everyone's greed."[40] They added, "Scientists are telling us that in the face of rising global population and increased energy and natural resource consumption, we have a limited 'window of opportunity' to change our environmentally destructive ways of relating to the earth. Failure to act in a timely and decisive manner will threaten the ability of the earth to nurture and sustain life as we know it."[41]

Responsibility for generations to come was advocated: "Our Christian ethic needs to expand to include an intergenerational ethic where the needs of future generations are included in present-day decisions."[42]

In conclusion, the Alberta bishops declared that "the eco-justice message of the biblical jubilee is a challenge for us to embrace a right relationship with God, all human beings and all creation."[43] Their words here recalled their earlier image of the "web of creation," and related to it ecological and economic justice.

Boston Province, United States, 2000:
And God Saw That It Was Good

The pastoral letter *And God Saw That It Was Good*[44] viewed environmental concerns in Maine, Vermont, New Hampshire, and Massachusetts through the lens of Catholic social teaching. In the Introduction, the regional bishops took up themes from Pope John Paul II by speaking about "the moral challenge of preserving the environment" and "the common vocation we all have as stewards of all God's creation," and by linking justice and environmental issues: "The promotion of human dignity cannot be separated from our care and protection of God's creation." They also local-ized these themes in their consideration of such issues as the need to ensure the economic health of their region's farms and fisheries to meet human needs for food and employment.[45]

The Boston Province bishops used "dominion" and "stew-ardship" interchangeably, even while noting how the former term has been used to harm creation, and called for intergenerational responsibility. They declared that people as God's images are "called to cooperate with God in the care of his creation. To have dominion, far from being a license to exploit and use the earth for selfish purposes, is to accept a sacred trust given to all humans to be responsible stewards of all that God has made."[46] Christians who are good stewards of creation demonstrate that they "know that theirs is not the final generation."[47]

The bishops offered several principles to guide Catholic attitudes and actions, including "respect for all of God's creation, heeding God's call to care for and be responsible for the goods of this world and its future"; "an ethical necessity for sharing this world's goods for the common good of all"; and "a preferential option for the poor."[48]

In contrast to institutional assertions that economics should determine the extent to which the environment should be protected, and to individualistic attitudes that evince a lack of concern for the needs of others, the bishops stated that "economic criteria alone cannot be the basis for a proper evaluation of the effects our behavior has on the environment. Moral evaluation is needed and corrective measures must be taken where needed."[49] They noted that "personal habits of overconsumption and waste have adverse environmental and social impacts. While some of us consume more than we need, others do not have enough to sustain life."[50]

Although the bishops did not write specifically about a "sacramental universe," they did advocate "the contemplation of God's goodness as manifested in creation."[51]

Columbia River International Bioregion, 2001:
The Columbia River Watershed: Caring for Creation and the Common Good

Environmental issues increasingly became a part of public consciousness in the U.S. Northwest and the Canadian Southwest in the past decade. Particular regional concerns included pollution from mining; pollution from chemicals from industrial plants, agricultural operations, and urban lawns; species extinction, particularly salmon in the Columbia and Snake rivers; and Native American fishing and treaty rights. The bishops of the Columbia River Watershed responded to these and other issues in their letter on ethical, economic, and ecological concerns of their region: *The Columbia River Watershed: Caring for Creation and the Common Good*.[52]

The pastoral letter had a bioregional focus (a first for a bishops' letter), which is a more ecologically and socially appropriate base for addressing issues not limited by state, provincial, or national boundaries. It was also an international document. The Columbia River's origin and the first four hundred of its twelve hundred miles are in Canada; and several dams constructed by treaty on the U.S.-Canadian border to provide U.S. energy companies with hydroelectric power have had adverse impacts in Canada on farmers, businesspeople, and rural communities. The bishops spoke throughout their document of steps toward a "spiritual, social and ecological transformation" of the watershed.

The document called people to be conscious of a community of place, of living in a space that is sacred because God-immanent blesses it. The local human community shares the watershed as its Earth home and is to care for it as their "common home"; the community is responsible for the creation in which it is situated.[53]

These responsibilities are embodied in human "stewardship" of creation (the word *dominion* is not used):

> Stewards, as caretakers for the things of God, are called to use wisely and distribute justly the goods of God's earth to meet the needs of God's children. They are to care for the earth as their home and as a beautiful revelation of the creativity, goodness and love of God. Creation is a "book of nature" in whose living pages people can see signs of the Spirit of God present in the universe, yet separate from it....Our unique role in creation as God's stewards carries with it a serious responsibility for service to God and to creation.[54]...Good stewards of creation use what they need and recognize that others, both those presently living and future generations, have a right to enjoy the fruits of the earth as well.[55]

Stewardship, then, is not just a consciousness of caring for the Earth in the present; it implies intergenerational responsibilities.

The bishops' letter referred obliquely to the "sacramental universe" described in the U.S. bishops' document *Renewing the Earth,* although the term itself was not used. Creation "is from God and reveals God," and can be "a sign and revelation for the person of faith, a moment of grace."[56] The universe and a local place, the commons, can be revelatory of God, since "signs of God's presence are evident in all of creation," and people open to the Spirit can experience this "loving presence."[57] In this passage, the "sacramental universe" became localized as a "sacramental commons"—again, without using the word *sacramental*.

Every commons has a possibility of meeting the needs of its human communities and the broader biotic community, but often the Earth and the goods of the Earth are reserved by and for a few. The bishops addressed these issues of land ownership and equitable distribution of Earth's benefits when they declared that "the commons belongs to everyone, and yet belongs to no one. We hold this land in trust for our present use, for future generations, and ultimately for God."[58]

Since the letter focused on the bioregion of the Columbia River and its tributaries, an area whose waters are afflicted by chemical and radioactive pollution and consequent extinction of salmon and other fish species, the bishops applied the biblical understanding of "living water" to their region.[59] God intends the Columbia River and its network of rivers to be "living water: bountiful and healthy providers for the common good. The water itself is to be a clear sign of the Creator's presence."[60]

As in other recent regional letters, the watershed bishops recognized that "social justice for people and proper respect for the earth are now seen as related issues."[61]

The bishops acknowledged "the inherent value of creation and the dignity of all living beings as creatures of God."[62] In doing so, they challenged the dominion perspective that creatures other than humans have merely an instrumental value, and are intended by God to be in the service of humanity.

The letter presented seven "Convictions That Underscore the Need to Care for the Earth":

1. God is the Creator of the universe and maintains its existence through an ongoing creative will.
2. God's presence is discernible in all creation.
3. God has blessed and called "very good" all that is created.
4. God loves the community of life.

5. God's creatures share a common home.
6. God entrusts the earth to human care. People are stewards of God's world.
7. God intends the earth's goods to be equitably shared.[63]

The sixth conviction reinforced the teaching that the Earth and its goods are held in "trust" by people; the Earth's benefits are not "gifts" (which could imply that they might be used by humanity independently of considerations about impacts on the Earth or effects on the human and biotic communities).

In their action proposals, the bishops offered ten "Considerations for Community Caretaking." The first is to "Consider the Common Good," so that "community and individual *needs* take priority over private *wants*. The right to own and use private property is not seen as an absolute individual right; this right must be exercised responsibly for the benefit of the owner and the community as a whole." Private property is "a trust from God to the civil owner." Public property should be viewed "as a community benefit to be conserved as a good both in itself and for what it can provide to meet human needs."[64] These ideas promote a sense of the inherent worth and sacredness of all creation.

In the other "considerations," the bishops advocated conservation of the watershed as a "common good"; wildlife protection; respect and justice for indigenous peoples, for the poor (noting the church's "option for the poor") and for distinctive ethnic and racial cultures; organic agricultural production; cooperative enterprises; recognition of people's "right to a clean and healthful environment"; and "establishment of environmentally integrated alternative energy sources." The letter included in an appendix a poetic reflection, "Riversong," which celebrated the peoples and places of the watershed and offered a vision of all creation living in a collaborative community.

The Columbia River Watershed environmental statement reinforced the significant shift in church attitudes toward ecological issues and humanity's place in the biotic community and its relation to the Earth as a whole, a shift that began to emerge in *Renewing the Earth* and was developed further in *At Home in the Web of Life.* While its advocacy of economic justice was not new, it did ameliorate anthropocentrism and taught instead that all members of the biotic community have an inherent goodness and value that should be respected; that people should relate well to other creatures and share with them a common Earth home viewed as a commons; and that "common good" understandings should be extended to non-human creation. Further, the word *dominion,* which has sometimes erroneously been used to justify "domination," was not used in the letter. Instead, there was a focus on "stewardship": human responsibility to care for creation as a trust from God.

In other regional letters, *dominion* was still used. Its problem as a theological term—that it could become, in the eyes of some, "domination"—was noted in *And God Saw That It Was Good,* which stated that "dominion" is not "a license to exploit and use the earth for selfish purposes" but rather "a sacred trust given to all humans to be responsible stewards."[65] While the latter pastoral still used *dominion,* it tempered the term with the more theocentric term *stewardship,* which put the concepts of hierarchy and human hegemony and control in a context of ultimate responsibility to God. The use of different terms in different letters indicates different stages of evolving Catholic environmental thought, or, in the words of the Appalachian bishops in 1995 in their section on Catholic Social Teaching, "the present state of this teaching" in particular areas.

Alaska Bishops, 2002: *A Catholic Perspective on Subsistence: Our Responsibility toward Alaska's Bounty and Our Human Family*

In Alaska, issues similar to those in the Columbia River Watershed prompted bishops there to state their environmental concerns.[66] A particular twist to the Alaska statement was discussion of the relationship of allocation of fish catches to subsistence needs of some groups in Alaska, notably communities of the rural poor and Native peoples.

The bishops noted the abundance of Earth's goods available to Alaskans, and then focused on the legal history and current state of discussion of subsistence issues in their state. They noted that while federal and state laws gave a subsistence priority for rural residents, the Alaska Supreme Court had later ruled that the Alaska Constitution "precluded the state from granting priority access to fish and wildlife based on place of residence."[67] A key issue addressed is "equal access to all" versus Native claims to resources dating back thousands of years and seemingly protected by the 1971 federal Alaska Native Claims Settlement Act.

The bishops observed that "'equal access' in itself does not guarantee a fair resolution."[68] They addressed several "moral implications of upholding equal access above all other values." The first was that "equal access is a means toward achieving the universal declaration of goods, not an end in and of itself. [Equal access sometimes] provides opportunity only to those most able to take advantage of the opportunity." They cited here a statement from Pope Paul VI that without solidarity, an overemphasis on equality can foster an individualism in which each person claims his or her rights without a concern for the common good. The second implication is that "equal treatment assumes that all citizens begin on equal footing with equal opportunity. Such is not the case in Alaska," since its original peoples did not formulate, but had to adapt to, later inhabitants' economic, judicial, and value systems. They declared that the constitutional enshrining of "equal access" when Alaska became a state "may have created an injustice for the Alaska native peoples." The third implication is that "unequal treatment can result from recognition that the circumstances of all people's lives are not identical, and sometimes those circumstances dictate disparate treatment." The bishops stated that a distinction must be made "between those policies that unjustly discriminate and those that require recognition of differences among peoples." They asserted that the former should be fought, and the latter developed to ensure justice.[69]

In the course of their discussion of these issues, the Alaska bishops offered insights from Catholic social teaching. They noted that several principles were applicable: solidarity, a preferential option for the poor, subsidiarity, care of creation, and the dignity of work. The bishops stated that human dignity and the common good are achieved only through community, which is developed through a sense of solidarity[70]

One aspect of solidarity related to the subsistence issue is "the requirement to show respect and honor for the culture and traditions of indigenous peoples," and therefore to protect the "right of the Alaska native people to preserve their cultures." The bishops observed the link between Alaska Natives' subsistence living, Earth-relatedness, and spirituality: "For thousands of years, the Alaska native peoples lived in a subsistence economy, drawing their human and spiritual values from the heritage of the land, the water and the wildlife." They noted great contributions made to Alaskan society by Native cultures, including "traditional perspectives on respect for creation and the family, and creative and powerful art and dance." They acknowledged that there was much cultural oppression and injustice committed against Native peoples, even by "Catholic leaders and teachers [who] contributed to that assault on the Alaska native cultures or failed to counter it."[71] (In contrast to the Catholic bishops and religious leaders of the northwestern United States, the Alaska bishops did not offer an apology for this.)

In discussing the "preferential option for the poor," the bishops offered the analogy that just as in a family a particular member might need for a time special attention from other family members, so, too, must the church focus attention on members of society most in need;[72] the poor in Alaska are such societal members.[73] What flows from this, the bishops asserted, is that a just allocation of resources, bearing in mind particular situations in which limitations of their acquisition are necessary in instances such as "to maintain sustainable fish and wildlife populations," people in greatest need must have priority of access. This and other subsistence opportunities "should be viewed not as charity, but as justice."[74]

The bishops discussed subsidiarity in terms of the benefits of local decision making, stating unqualifiedly that "the principle of subsidiarity and the prudential judgment of most Alaskans favor a return of management to state government with local participation."[75] (Unfortunately, while this was obviously a reaction against some failed federal policies, it contradicted the bishops' earlier statement that federal and state laws tried to assure subsistence to Native peoples, but that the Alaska Supreme Court overturned those on the basis of the Court's interpretation of the Alaska Constitution "equal access" provision. Also, the Native peoples are a minority in most communities, and a "local determination" of an issue such as fishing rights might result in continued exclusion of Native fishers from local waters. The Columbia River situation already described illustrates this: the states of Washington and Oregon, as well as the federal government, ocean fishing corporations, and river commercial and sport fishers controlled the fishing on the Columbia. Native peoples could only catch fish in the last upriver zone after all of the preceding non-Indian commercial operations and individuals had exercised their "legal rights," as determined primarily locally.)

In their discussion of stewardship, the bishops declared that "subsistence, by any definition, concerns the just stewardship of the fish and wildlife resources provided by the Creator."[76] (Although "stewardship" implied a trust from the Creator, viewing living creatures as "resources" expressed more of a domination or dominion perspective, and additional anthropocentrism occurred in the idea that these "resources" are provided to humans by the Creator, which can imply that they are not good in themselves in the Creator's view. Here again was an instance where the concept of the "universal destination of goods," when limited solely to goods being destined for humans, clashed with the teaching that all of creation is pronounced "good" by the Creator who loves all creatures.) A few paragraphs later the bishops declared that people living at the subsistence level "have a particularly unique relationship with nature. Through their daily natural connection with the land and the work, they experience creation and, with their Creator, proclaim, 'It is good.' The traditional belief in Alaska native cultures that the animals offer themselves to the hunter, that they 'sacrifice themselves,' engenders a unique respect and reverence for the animals." They added that "God endowed nature with a wondrous power to communicate God's presence, power and beauty. Future regulations must not deprive God's children of the opportunity to learn and seek inspiration from creation."[77] (Here again are signs of an environmental theology in development, where contradictory ideas are presented without noting their relationship to each other. Traditional anthropocentric theology cannot be integrated with newer understandings of the goodness of creation and creatures, a sense of the Creator's immanence in creation, and recognition that the Creator loves creatures in and for themselves, not just because they can be instrumental to humankind. Traditional concern for the most vulnerable members of the human family can and has been integrated with environmental theology, however: the vulnerable of the human community and the threatened and endangered members of the biotic community as a whole can be respected, and steps taken to affirm their dignity and to provide for their needs.)

In the various considerations cited in the regional and local bishops' statements, the "sacramental universe" and the affirmation of the rights of Native peoples merit special attention. The former is a theological and spiritual understanding with practical implications. The latter represents an instance in which the church stands with a minority group that often lacks the economic resources, social status, and political power to assert its human rights.

4
Transforming Tradition and Conserving Creation: Northern Visions

In the Americas, three decades of environmental conscious-ness in the broader culture during the latter part of the twentieth century stimulated theological consideration of the role that the Christian religion has played and might play in relation to ecolog-ical issues. Connections between theology and ecology have been made not only in official Catholic Church documents, such as those cited previously, but also—and, sometimes, more impor-tantly because of their proponents' direct engagement with envi-ronmental movements and issues—by independent Catholic thinkers. Some of the insights of these authors have been at the forefront in stimulating new understandings of human relation-ships to the Earth's environment.

People described in this chapter (and the following chapter) emerged from the Catholic tradition, reflected on it, and explored its meaning within the natural and social historical contexts of a dynamic universe, an evolving Earth, and developing human communities. Some would stretch and even break this connection with the institutional Catholic Church, while retaining their rela-tionship with the universal community of Christian believers.

Analysis of the church documents cited in previous chapters reveals that shifts in understanding—some gradual, some more abrupt—have occurred in some aspects of Catholic thought on environmental issues, on humans' relation to creation, and on awareness of the immanence of God in creation and the concrete implications of that awareness. Such shifts should not be seen as startling, since all traditions have a specific historical origin in the awareness and capability of people of a particular social context. Theological thought, beyond basic core beliefs, is, to adapt the *Catechism*'s description of creation, *in statu viae:* in a state of becoming, not a finished product. In environmental theology, "domination" has given way to "dominion," which has been superseded to some extent by "stewardship." Developments in theology once seen as "radical" eventually became doctrines, and old ways of thinking about the universe have changed: consider the impacts of Galileo Galilei and Charles Darwin, for example.

Visionary voices, then, offer new insights that might or might not eventually be incorporated in the long term, but deserve presentation and consideration: to stimulate further developments in theology-ecology understandings, or to help people to clarify current understandings—or both. In this and other areas, a dynamic theology open to the guidance of the Spirit retains core beliefs but surrenders historically and culturally limited understandings not central to the core.

The thinkers that follow address a variety of issues relative to ecological integrity and Christian faith-based environmental concern and action. In some cases, those reflecting on the theology-ecology interface in the years ending the twentieth century and beginning the twenty-first restated ideas expressed in Catholic circles earlier in the twentieth century by American Indian/Native American[1] Catholics, who fused traditions thousands of years old in the Americas with the newer Christian tradition.

Prologue: Black Elk and Fools Crow—
Weaving Lakota and Catholic Traditions

In the nineteenth century, as Euro-Americans pushed westward and forcefully displaced Indian peoples, Christianity was instilled in these Native nations because of religious fervor or to coerce their inculturation into European modes of thinking. Catholic missionaries were among the Christian emissaries who sought to alter the indigenous, Earth-related spirituality. In some cases, those who were baptized into the new worldview did not reject entirely their "old ways." Among the latter were two noted spiritual leaders and healers from the Lakota (Sioux) Nation: Black Elk (1863–1950) and Fools Crow (1890–1989), whose lives bridged the nineteenth and twentieth centuries. Both spiritual leaders sought to integrate their old traditions with the new teachings of the Catholic Church. Fools Crow related how Black Elk, who had become interested in Catholicism, told him that "he had decided that the Sioux religious way of life was pretty much the same as that of the Christian churches, and there was no reason to change what the Sioux were doing. We could pick up some of the Christian ways and teachings, and just work them in with our own, so in the end both would be better."[2]

Black Elk (1863–1950)

Beginning in the twentieth century, numerous New Age adherents have sought to appropriate American Indian spirituality, often while rejecting Christian beliefs and practices. Few people realize that an Indian elder perceived in Native circles and beyond as a traditional leader and healer, the Lakota known as Hehaka Sapa—Black Elk—was also a Catholic.

Baptized Nicholas and usually called "Nick," Black Elk was made famous in the non-Native world through poet John G. Neihardt's 1932 publication of *Black Elk Speaks*.[3] Born in about 1863, Black Elk had his "Great Vision" in 1872, when he was

nine years old. In the vision he was taught that he would hold varied respected roles among his people. Eventually, he became a
healer, a warrior (he was a cousin of Crazy Horse), a horse trainer
for Buffalo Bill's Wild West Show, and a visionary holy man. He
was baptized a Catholic in 1904, and later served as a paid cate-
chist to his people on behalf of Jesuit missionaries for some thirty
years. His conversion was linked in his mind to a vision he had
experienced many years earlier, in 1890, when he participated in
a ghost dance at Wounded Knee Creek near Manderson, South
Dakota. In this vision, he saw a man standing against the tree of
life with arms outstretched, bathed in a golden light and accompanied by twelve men. The man, who had an eagle feather (sym-
bolic of a leader who serves as a messenger from the Spirit to the
people) in his long hair, spoke to him. (Black Elk said that he had
this vision before he had had much contact with Christians. He
told Neihardt[4] that he thought he had truly seen the son of the
Great Spirit in this vision.) He was a delegate to the Catholic
Sioux Indian Congress numerous times, and is pictured there in
photos taken in 1911, 1920, and 1946. He was known as a good
orator among his people. He was featured on the front cover of
the *Indian Sentinel,* the Bureau of Catholic Indian Missions fund-
raising magazine, in 1926. Although he never publicly performed
religious ceremonies after he became a Catholic, he retained his
traditional spiritual perspective, which made him an effective cat-
echist among his people. He was the godfather to numerous children when they were baptized into the church.

Black Elk's teachings, given in interviews when he was
already a Catholic, offer insights useful for Christian ecological
consciousness. He told Joseph Epes Brown:

> But perhaps the most important reason for "lamenting" ["cry-
> ing for a vision" or *Hanblecheyapi,* one of the seven sacred
> rites of the Lakota] is that it helps us to realize our oneness
> with all things, to know that all things are our relatives; and
> then in behalf of all things we pray to *Wakan-Tanka* that He

may give to us knowledge of Him who is the source of all things, yet greater than all things.[5]

Black Elk related that a "lamenter" heard a bird tell him to "be attentive as you walk!" This meant that he should always be mindful of *Wakan-Tanka,* the Great Spirit, as he journeys through life, and watchful for signs given to him by *Wakan-Tanka.*[6]

In describing the Sun Dance, Black Elk observes (in words reminiscent of Psalm 148 and Saint Francis's *Canticle of All Creatures*) that "even in the very lightest breeze you can hear the voice of the cottonwood tree [in the center of the dance circle]; this we understand is its prayer to the Great Spirit, for not only men, but all things and all beings pray to Him continually in differing ways."[7]

Black Elk teaches that the Lakota have a strong sense of the interrelatedness of all beings in creation: "We know that we are related and are one with all things of the heavens and the earth, and we know that all the things that move are a people as we."[8] He describes later the peace "which comes within the souls of men when they realize their relationship, their oneness, with the universe and all its Powers, and when they realize that at the center of the universe dwells *Wakan-Tanka,* and that this center is really everywhere, it is within each of us."[9]

Black Elk integrated traditional Lakota spirituality and Christian beliefs as related perspectives on sacred reality. His life and work remain an inspiration not only for contemporary Native people who search for their own cultural identity and seek traditional spiritual insights that emerge from it, but also for Christians who strive to integrate core traditional doctrines with an appreciation of the immanence of the Creator in creation.

Fools Crow (1890–1989)

Fools Crow's life overlapped, in part, that of Black Elk, and they knew and respected each other as friends and relatives: Fools Crow was Black Elk's nephew. As was the case with Black Elk,

Fools Crow's life and teachings were brought before a world audience by a writer from the dominant culture, in this case Thomas E. Mails, a Lutheran priest, ethnographer, writer, and artist who befriended and interviewed Fools Crow and completed the book *Fools Crow* in 1979.

Fools Crow on several occasions describes his relationship with Black Elk. He related to Mails that "my uncle, the renowned Black Elk, has earned a place above all of the other Teton holy men....All he wanted to do was love and serve his fellow man....I learned a great deal about *Wakan-Tanka,* prophecy and medicine from him."[10] He also knew that Black Elk had become a Catholic. After consulting with his uncle, Fools Crow was baptized in 1917. Six decades later he related that "I am still a practicing Roman Catholic....At the same time, we live according to the traditional religious beliefs and customs of our people, and we find few problems with the differences between the two. Many things we believe about God are the same."[11] Fools Crow saw a similarity between Sun Dance piercings (flesh offerings by the dancers, who are tied to the center tree with ropes attached with wooden pegs to their chest, and dance back from the tree to pull them out) and Jesus' offering on the cross: "Since the white man has come to us and explained how God sent his own son to be sacrificed, we realize that our sacrifice is similar to Jesus' own."[12]

On the day in 1974 when Mails first met Fools Crow to propose a book, a thunderstorm raged about the community center in Kyle, South Dakota, in which they met, threatening to force cancellation of a weekend fair that raised funds for social programs on the Pine Ridge reservation. A local leader brought a filled sacred pipe to Fools Crow and asked "Grandfather" (a term of respect for an elder) if he would split the rain clouds (send them around a particular place); it was known that Fools Crow, and a few other elders, had been granted this intercessory power. Fools Crow went out and prayed, and told the people not to worry. Overnight the storm abated, and by morning, the sky above and around the site of the fair was clear. Mails relates that by nine o'clock "people were set-ting up their displays. The clouds were split!"[13]

Fools Crow had no formal education, and spoke little Eng-lish, but had no regrets for his "lack of White schooling," seeing himself as far richer spiritually and in fulfilling "the role I have been given."[14] Like Black Elk, he traveled with Buffalo Bill's Wild West Show. He was a man of peace who had been told by his spiritual teacher that he was not to go to war or even have a per-sonal fight with anyone. Fools Crow became a medicine man in 1913, and was called to the greater role of holy man in 1914. He began his healing work in 1920.[15]

Whenever he was asked to heal, Fools Crow would set aside whatever he was doing and respond to the need at hand. He healed without requiring recompense, although he was permitted to accept gifts expressing gratitude. Throughout his life, his cere-monies were never known to fail. He did not regard his extraordi-nary powers as inherent: he saw himself as a Sun Dance eagle bone whistle through which the Creator breathed; he was a chan-nel through whom flowed the power of the Spirit. He observed that "you have to be a good person and in the right spirit before the spirit powers can and will help you."[16]

In a time of diminishing Earth goods ("resources") and an expanding population on the reservation, Fools Crow's father told him that while everyone agreed that it was wonderful to have children, "if the children were to be healthy and cared for, they should be limited in number to what their parents could handle well," and that "with a restricted amount of land available they could not support an unlimited population."[17]

Fools Crow lived simply, dedicated to his multiple roles as ceremonial chief, district leader, human rights activist, spiritual leader, mediator, Sun Dance leader, and family man. In 1975, he became the first Indian holy man to offer the opening prayer for the U.S. Senate.

As was the case with Black Elk, Fools Crow's spirituality was a fusion of traditional Lakota beliefs and Catholic teachings, all related to a deep relationship with the Creator and a profound respect for the Earth and all living creatures. This spirituality was expressed through frequent prayer every day, and use of the sacred pipe for particular times of reflection and prayer.

The traditional Lakota way of life, according to Fools Crow, had three elements: to love family, relatives, and friends; to understand and relate closely to nature; and to thank *Wakan-Tanka* for all that was given.[18]

In his own life, Fools Crow lived daily in the spirit of those elements. He integrated his Creator-creation spirituality with his Catholic beliefs, all within the context of his relationship with his people's community and with the community of all life.

Catholicism and Indigenous Traditions

During much of Black Elk's lifetime, and even into the present, Christian churches have been engaged in intense missionary efforts to convert Indians to Christianity, efforts aided by U.S. government policies. Sacred places were destroyed, and many artifacts that did not suffer a similar fate were sent to museums or to commercial enterprises for sale to tourists and collectors. In recent years, the Catholic Church and other Christian churches have begun to explore more openly the interaction of indigenous peoples' Mother Earth-related spirituality with Christian ideas about and attitudes toward creation.[19] As seen earlier, Pope John Paul II has supported Native peoples' spirituality and environmental consciousness (chapter 2) and the U.S. bishops issued a statement in 1992 affirming Indian culture and spirituality (chapter 3). A similar respect for indigenous traditions and appreciation of their spiritual insights led several theologians to incorporate in their writings a complementary creation-focused spiritual and theological consciousness.

Matthew Fox: God's Original Blessing

Matthew Fox developed an innovative theological approach to the relations between people and Earth in *Original Blessing,* where he presented his ideas on "creation-centered spirituality."

Fox believes that the Christian tradition has focused too strongly on fall/redemption theology and spirituality. He rejects the fall/redemption approach to human relations with God and the cosmos as a dualistic and patriarchal model that "does not teach believers about the New Creation or creativity, about justice-making and social transformation…, fails to teach love of the earth or care for the cosmos…[and] fails to listen to the impassioned pleas of the *anawim,* the little ones, of human history."[20] For Fox, "to teach original sin and never to teach original blessing creates pessimism and cynicism."[21] Since the history of the universe is billions of years older than human history, and human sinfulness is therefore a relatively recent occurrence, and since God blessed God's creation from the moment of its emergence,[22] then a universe spirituality, recognizing and participating in God's original blessing, should replace a human spirituality focused on the fall/redemption teaching. He declares that "original blessing is prior to any sin, original or less than original."[23] The original sin focus has been key in separating humans from the rest of creation and the Creator.[24]

What follows necessarily from Fox's focus on original blessing is a reconsideration of the meaning of the incarnation and understandings of who Jesus is and what is his role among us in creation. Fox states that "Jesus, who is a new creation, calls all persons to reconciliation with themselves, with one another, and with creation."[25]

Problems of imperfection and suffering in the universe result from the universe still being in a process of being created: "In nature, in creation, imperfection is not a sign of the absence of God. It is a sign that the ongoing creation is no easy thing."[26] God is not detached from, but shares in the pain of Earth's creatures.

God permeates creation, is ever-present within creation, and is involved in an ongoing creation:

> There is one flow, one divine energy, one divine word in the sense of one creative energy flowing through all things, all time, all space, We are part of that flow and we need to listen to it rather than to assume arrogantly that our puny words are the only words of God.[27]...A creation-centered spirituality is cosmic....We are in the cosmos and the cosmos is in us.[28]

In this panentheistic perspective, people understand that "God is in everything and everything is in God." Through panentheism, creation-centered spirituality "experiences God." Panentheism sees the world "sacramentally," for "the primary sacrament is creation itself," from which "other sacraments derive their fruitful and creative power."[29] The "sacramental universe" suggested by the U.S. bishops in *Renewing the Earth* finds a complementary expression here, though not in terms precisely offered (or apt to be accepted) by the bishops. Fox shifts away from traditional church teachings about the sacraments and their origins, following here his own suggestion that in theology, creation should have primacy over fall/redemption.

In *Creation Spirituality* Fox carries forward his major themes and adds new ideas about a creation-based spirituality. After observing that science has developed new insights about the nature of the universe, he suggests the need for a new creation story that would also be a "new story of history. It places humanity's history within the context of the history of the cosmos itself."[30] Such a spirituality "insists not just on justice among humans but on geo-justice—justice between humans and the earth and all her creatures,"[31] and "empowers us for an ecological era, a time when we cease looking *up* for divinity and start looking *around*."[32] He leaves open the possibility that not only humans will have new life: "Perhaps Jesus' being raised from the dead is what divinity does to all it creates. Perhaps, after all, no beauty is lost in the universe."[33]

While Fox advocates social justice for humans, his emphasis is on individual self-transformation rather than communal social transformation: "While institutional criticism is certainly called for, much change must come from within individuals' psyches and ways of perceiving the world....No group can liberate another group. People liberate themselves."[34] He does call for a shift from "an anthropocentric and nondemocratic capitalism to an Earth-centered economics," however, because of the environmental devastation caused by capitalism,[35] and he calls on "the peoples of the Americas to look more closely at one another's history, to see one another's struggles in light of their own, and to begin to work together."[36]

Matthew Fox suggests significant changes for environmental theology. In fact, he would prefer to speak of a "creation-centered spirituality" rather than a theology. His visions both for religious thought and for creation's transformation provide new insights for Christians, in particular, who are reflecting on their relationship to creation. His somewhat individualistic focus would appeal more to New Age adherents and individualist Christians than to socially activist Christians, but his concept of "original blessing" and his reflections that flow from it should stimulate reflection and insights from a broad spectrum of people interested in Spirit–human–creation relationships.

Rosemary Radford Ruether: Ecofeminism and Ecojustice

A new dimension in environmental thought emerged in the writings of ecofeminists. In the Catholic tradition, an important contributor from this perspective is Rosemary Radford Ruether, whose *Gaia and God* presents rich insights into the relationship of religion and ecology.

Ruether notes that "ecofeminism...explores how male domination of women and domination of nature are interconnected," and declares that "a healed relation to the earth...demands a social reordering to bring about just and loving interrelationship between men and women, between races and nations, between groups presently stratified into social classes, manifest in great disparities of access to the means of life....We must speak of eco-justice."[37]

Classical Western cultural traditions, including Christianity, "have justified and sacralized these relationships of domination."[38] These traditions did, however, struggle "with what they perceived to be injustice and sin and sought to create just and loving relations between people in their relation to the earth and to the divine," and "there are also glimpses in this heritage of transformative, biophilic relationships."[39] Ruether thereby places herself among those who would seek to transform the tradition rather than reject it and start over in human–Earth relationships with a profoundly different religious orientation; she observes, for example, that "merely replacing a male transcendent deity with an immanent female one is an insufficient answer to the 'god-problem.'"[40] On the other hand, she sees the need for a reformation of existing traditions, since "there is no ready-made ecological spirituality and ethic in past traditions."[41]

Ruether states that "deep repentance needs to happen among the powerful of the earth,"[42] and that *metanoia* is needed: "conversion of our spirit and culture, of our technology and social relations, so that the human species exists within nature in a life-sustaining way."[43] These themes resonate well with contemporary Catholic Church social teachings on economic justice and environmental responsibility.

In the Genesis 2 creation story, the narrative, while anthropocentric, does not intend an "exploitative or destructive rule over earth," since Earth's ultimate ownership remains God's, and people as God's stewards would not fulfill their role if they were to act destructively.[44] Humans as stewards have a unique responsibility to God and creation, as represented in the teaching that people are "images of God" into whose hands care of the Earth is entrusted.[45] Humans as stewards have a covenantal relationship to all life, and are "caretakers who did not create and do not absolutely own the rest of life, but who are ultimately accountable for its welfare to the true source of life, God."[46]

In the biotic community, "one of the most basic 'lessons' of ecology for ethics and spirituality is the interrelation of all things."[47] When species are destroyed, "pages of the book of life are being ripped out before we have even had a chance to read them."[48] Species are not just on Earth for humans, "species have their own intrinsic value in themselves and as members of biotic communities."[49] Extinction of just one species means that "whole communities of interdependent plants, animals, and insects are being wiped out. The result is a degraded whole."[50]

Asceticism is to be understood not as a world-negating, body-disciplining practice focused on transcendence and an after-life, "but rather as a rejection of exploitation and excess, and thus as a return to egalitarian simple living in harmony with other humans and with nature."[51]

The linkage of ecology and justice is seen in the biblical tradition that teaches about a single "lived reality in time and place that is not differentiated into separate spheres of 'creation' and 'redemption.' The God made present in historical acts of deliverance is at the same time the God who 'made heaven and earth.'"[52] Thus, while some might make a distinct break between caring for creation and concern for community, Ruether sees them as inseparably linked in the unified acts of God. She notes later that the Logos-Christ is "the power of the new creation" and "the principle through which this cosmos was originally created and now is renewed and reconciled with God."[53]

People should envision a good society, whose foundational principle is equity: gender equity, regional human groups' equity, global equity among human communities, equity among all members of the biotic community, and intergenerational equity among all living beings.[54]

Human population growth is a concern. Species sometimes have such a drive to live and expand that they "proliferate in a cancerous way," and endanger or even destroy the context of their existence. The life force is "evil" when a species maximizes itself at others' expense; the "good" lies in "limits," in a balancing of the drives for life of all members in a biotic community.[55] Planetary survival requires not only a decline in humans' consumption of Earth's goods; "a significant curbing and eventual reduction of human population itself is also necessary."[56] This will come to pass through means such as the "promotion of effective birth control on a widespread basis sufficient to halt and reduce the world population explosion," the "empowerment of women as moral agents of their own sexuality and reproduction," and "a double transformation of both women and men in their relation to each other and to 'nature.'"[57]

In a later work she edited, *Women Healing Earth,* Ruether reaffirms her ecofeminist stance and takes to task to some extent First World ecofeminists who focus on goddess worship based in past religious practice as a means of overcoming ten millennia of patriarchy, but do not "examine and take responsibility for their actual social context as heirs and beneficiaries of this conquest as First World affluent people. Many essentialist or matricentric Northern ecofeminists fail to make real connections between their own reality as privileged women and racism, classism, and impoverishment of nature." In order for Northern ecofeminism not to be "primarily a cultural escapism for an affluent female elite [it] must make concrete connections with women at the bottom of the social-economic system."[58]

Rosemary Ruether accents the social dimensions of environmental theology, in contrast to the more individual perspective of Matthew Fox. They share in common a great respect for creation and a sense that humans are to care for creation as members of an interdependent and interrelated community of life.

Daniel Maguire: Population Pressures

Population growth has a significant impact on the environment. Official Catholic Church documents address the issue, but with qualifiers limiting options for couples. Within the Catholic tradition, Daniel C. Maguire offers insights suggesting expansion of church understandings and teachings, based upon a reassessment of the institutional church position on permissible options.

In *Ethics for a Small Planet,* a book he co-authored with Larry Rasmussen, Maguire notes that there is a 1.6 percent annual increase in the global human population, putting a strain on Earth's ability to provide for human needs.[59] The resulting human impoverishment especially harms women and children. Maguire observes, "Women constitute 70 percent of the world's 1.3 billion poor, own less than 1 percent of the world's property but work two thirds of the world's working hours."[60] He also states that "it took 10,000 generations to reach the first 2 1/2 billion; it took one generation to double it," and that 90 percent of population growth is in the world's poorest areas.[61] Increases in the population strain Earth's ability to provide for people's needs. Maguire finds in the Catholic tradition, in the writings of Thomas Aquinas, support for limiting population growth—even to the extent of using government efforts to do so:

> Thomas agreed with Aristotle that the number of children generated should not exceed the resources of the community and that this should be ensured by law as needed....He did not shrink from the need for the state to limit birth. If more than a determined number of citizens were generated, he said, the result would be poverty which would breed thievery, sedition, and chaos.[62]

Maguire states later his own view on government involvement in population issues. The requirements of the common good sometimes necessitate restrictions on personal rights. Since government's purpose is to protect the common good and the well-being of the disempowered, it might need to make and enforce laws about reproductive choices if individual conscience and voluntarism are not exercised responsibly when making reproductive choices, thereby threatening the capability of humans and other members of the biotic community to survive and thrive.[63]

Unlike some Northern Hemisphere government officials and their supporters in academe, Maguire does not blame the population growth among the poor in the Southern Hemisphere as the sole cause for ecological devastation and shortage of Earth's goods. In *Visions of a New Earth: Religious Perspectives on Population, Consumption, and Ecology,* which he co-edited with Harold Coward, Maguire declares that "concern for human numbers without concern for overconsuming elites is unjust and unhelpful. A single superconsumer in the rich world does more harm to the earth than hundreds of the poor."[64]

Maguire is concerned that some faith communities are not open to new perspectives on the sacred, which are necessary for a responsible relation of people and their world. The "Abrahamic religions," he states, "are notoriously unopen to dialogue about their beliefs," displaying "rigidity," an "overconfident dogmatism," and a "simplistic sureness."[65]

As an example, Maguire cites Christianity for its frequent focus on human life on Earth as a preparation for an otherworldly existence after death, so that the value of Earth is seen as secondary and "biocentricity gives way to theocentricity."[66] Hope for an afterlife, then, "might do more than opiate the social conscience"; it can also "make our earth-life the prologue, not the text and context of our being."[67] This does not bode well for the well-being of the Earth: "Earth as main stage becomes earth as prelude: the biological may be seen as hostile to the spiritual. At the least, its status is diminished. It is not our home but the proving ground for our real home beyond. That is troubling news for the rest of nature."[68]

Daniel Maguire, then, has a particular focus on population issues and on valuing human earthly existence in itself. He suggests that Earth and all life will be harmed if human population growth and the related increased human overconsumption of available Earth goods are not curtailed. His exposition of human population issues is more strongly and extensively expressed than in other writers emerging from the Catholic tradition. While the majority view, like the majority vote, is not always the morally correct stance, it does represent a breadth of thinking in a particular place and time. Maguire's position, while at variance with official church teachings, is representative of the perspectives of many, if not most, of the general public, Catholic or not. Increasingly greater numbers of Catholics not directly under the authority of church officials are openly and frequently expressing similar views. Some might be more concerned than Maguire appears to be about coercive government efforts (such as those in China), but equally supportive of educational efforts in such areas as sex education and promotion of sexual responsibility. In any case, this issue, not often discussed in church settings and church documents, is becoming more a part of concerned public discourse, particularly among the laity.

Thomas Berry: Ecotheology

Thomas Berry has been for more than twenty years a leading voice in contemporary efforts to promote Catholic consciousness of the immanence of the Spirit in creation. A Passionist priest for whom 2002 marked the sixtieth anniversary of ordination, he studied religions from around the world and came to understand and appreciate that peoples of diverse cultures and time periods have a religious and spiritual consciousness of divine presence. He describes the extraordinary beauty of dynamic creation, and links his experience with his childhood perceptions of what he would later call the "numinous presence" of the Spirit in the world and the cosmos.

In his writings Berry articulates his appreciation of the numinous, and suggests that such an appreciation would be helpful in restoring a balanced relationship between humans and the other creatures of their Earth habitat, and with the cosmos beyond. He sees creation as a community: "Especially in the realm of living beings there is an absolute interdependence."[69]

Humans must acknowledge this, because "the future can exist only when we understand the universe as composed of subjects to be communed with, not as objects to be exploited."[70]

Berry declares that humankind must be integrated with the dynamics of the cosmos. To achieve this integration is a "Great Work," a significant historical movement that gives "shape and meaning to life."[71]

Berry states that the basis of this work is acknowledgment that "the human and other components of Earth form a single community of life....Every mode of being has inherent rights to their place in this community, rights that come by existence itself."[72] In other words, not just humankind and other living creatures have rights, but Earth as well: "Every being has rights to be recognized and revered. Trees have tree rights, insects have insect rights, rivers have river rights, mountains have mountain rights. So too with the entire range of beings throughout the universe. All rights are limited and relative. So too with humans. We have human rights."[73] The rights of all nature, in a context of the extraordinary power that people have over nature, must be legally established if Earth is to survive;[74] this jurisprudence would acknowledge the legal rights of abiotic and biotic aspects of Earth, and include protection for habitat as sacred and inviolable.[75] In this way, evolving biosystems could "be themselves"[76] and "every component of the Earth community would have its rights in accord with the proper mode of its being and its functional role."[77] Earth should, in fact, "be viewed primarily as an interrelated system of bioregions, and only secondarily as a community of nations."[78] People need to move from democracy to "biocracy"; Earth needs "a United Species, not simply a United Nations."[79]

Berry deplores anthropocentrism, which permeates people's perceptions of both material and spiritual realities: "Even when we recognize the spirit world beyond the human we make everything referent to the human as the ultimate source of meaning and of value."[80] Humans' "radically anthropocentric society" has "broken the primary law of the universe, the law of the integrity of the universe, the law that every component member of the universe should be integral with every other member of the universe and that the primary norm of reality and of value is the universe community itself in its various forms of expression."[81]

While people should not be anthropocentric, the human is unique as "that being in whom the universe celebrates itself and its numinous origins in a special mode of conscious self-awareness."[82] Humans "activate one of the deepest dimensions of the universe."[83] The "anthropic principle" means for Berry that "the human is that being in whom the universe comes to itself in a special mode of conscious reflection."[84] In contrast to an EarthFirst! perspective that humans contribute nothing to life on Earth, Berry asserts that in the evolutionary process humankind is unique and would not have survived if it had not had a basic role in the Earth community.[85]

There is a web of relatedness that makes the dynamic, diverse, and complex cosmos a "universe" in which "everything is intimately present to everything else….Nothing is completely itself without everything else. This relatedness is both spatial and temporal. However distant in space or time, the bond of unity is functionally there. The universe is a communion and a community. We ourselves are that communion become conscious of itself."[86] In words reminiscent of the findings of quantum physics, Berry observes that "every reality of the universe is intimately present to every other reality of the universe and finds its fulfillment in this mutual presence,"[87] and "nothing in the universe could be itself apart from every other being in the universe, nor could any moment of the universe story exist apart from all the other moments in the story."[88]

Thomas Berry laments Christians' loss of a sense of the sacred; the natural world over time came to be viewed "primarily for 'use' rather than as manifestation of some numinous presence."[89] The sense of wonder and of the sacred will be recovered only if people view the universe "as a revelatory experience of that numinous presence whence all things come into being." For Berry (as for Fox), "the universe is the primary sacred reality," and people "become sacred by our participation in this more sublime dimension of the world about us."[90] People should realize that "the spiritual and the physical are two dimensions of the single reality that is the universe itself."[91] This reality comes to be understood in ways not subject to the limitations of religious statements in the Bible or other sacred writings, or of scientific explorations, theories, or discoveries. In fact, "emphasis on verbal revelation to neglect of the manifestation of the divine in the natural world is to mistake the entire revelatory process."[92] The revelatory experience will not require any "telescope, microscope, or scientific analysis."[93]

Indigenous peoples have a particular sense of the sacred. Their presence "to the numinous powers of this continent expressed through its natural phenomena expresses an ancient spiritual identity....To be allied with these powers is primary and necessary for every significant human endeavor on this continent."[94] The natural world has been "the manifestation of a numinous presence that gave meaning to all existence."[95]

The universe is less a "cosmos" than a *cosmogenesis,* "a universe ever coming into being through an irreversible sequence of transformations moving, in the larger arc of its development, from a lesser to a great order of complexity and from a lesser to a great consciousness."[96] This universe did not come into being on its own, but emerged "through some originating source beyond human comprehension."[97] (Berry's ideas here complement the *Catholic Catechism* statement, seen in chapter 1, that creation is *in statu viae.*)

The Earth as a whole and in its component parts, both living and nonliving, should be seen as, and become, a *commons.* In this complex of related beings, "each individual being is supported by every other being in the earth community. In turn, each being contributes to the well-being of every other being in the community."[98] Berry complements ideas offered by Rosemary Ruether when he states that "when we destroy the living forms of this planet...we destroy modes of divine presence."[99] He believes that humans need the variety of living beings on Earth primarily to meet "a psychic, rather than a physical, need."[100]

The sense of the spiritual that people experience in the natural world is not solely an engagement with divine immanence, and people who limit their experience to that possibility may be drawn away "from the sacred dimension of the earth in itself. This is not exactly the divine presence." People step beyond "the merely physical order of things to the divine presence in things." This is important, but so also is it necessary to "develop a sense of the reality and nobility of the natural world in itself."[101] Just as a certain type of spirituality intellectually might leap beyond the spiritual reality of the natural world to a perception solely of divine immanence, an "identification of the divine as transcendent to the natural world," while making a "direct human-divine covenant relationship possible," would "negate the natural world as the locus for the meeting of the divine and the human."[102] (Thus, a sense of God-immanent and a sense of God-transcendent both can lead people away from the spirit of the Earth—Earth's numinous reality—even while leading them toward the Spirit of the Earth—divine reality.)

Berry believes that a recovery of the sense of the sacred in the natural world as a "primary revelation of the divine" would rightly "diminish our emphasis on redemption experience in favor of a greater emphasis on creation processes. Creation, however, must now be experienced as the emergence of the universe as a psychic-spiritual as well as a material-physical reality from the beginning. We need to see ourselves as integral with this emergent process, as that being in whom the universe reflects on and celebrates itself."[103]

Human explorations of the dimensions of reality are to include participation in what Berry calls "the dream of the Earth," its "inherent powers in bringing forth this marvelous display of beauty in such unending profusion, a display so overwhelming to human consciousness that we might very well speak of it as being dreamed into existence." Human dreams of a better world "can only be distant expressions of this primordial source of the universe itself in its full extent in space and in the long sequence of its transformations in time."[104] Berry suggests that people at times might "participate in the original dream of the earth. Perhaps there are times when this primordial design becomes visible," and can provide humanity with "the guidance needed for the task that is before us."[105]

In an age when reductionist science seeks solely physical explanations of the dynamics of the universe and the evolution of the biotic community, Berry declares that "beyond our genetic coding, we need to go to the earth, as the source whence we came, and ask for its guidance, for the earth carries the psychic structure as well as the physical form of every living being upon the planet." Beyond the Earth, people must "go to the universe," which "carries the deep mysteries of our existence within itself." In the universe, people will encounter a vision and power greater than anything that human thought or culture might develop.[106]

Thomas Berry offers a unique and perceptive spiritual and social analysis of the relationship of humankind to the community of life, to the Earth as a whole, to the universe in which these are situated, and to the Spirit who has brought all of this into being. The Spirit's immanent presence in creation can be experienced as a complement to the spiritual dimension inherent in creation.

John Haught: Creation and Evolution

A primary focus of the work of John Haught in recent years has been the engagement of religion and science, and his proposals for a "theology of evolution."[107] While his emphasis has been on the implications for theology and religion of the ideas of Charles Darwin and of Neo-Darwinians such as E. O. Wilson, Daniel Dennett, and Richard Dawkins, Haught has explored within that emphasis ideas about human interaction with Earth and members of the biotic community.[108] In his writings, he utilizes process philosophy and process theology as bases to explore the human–creation relationship.

Haught views nature as "promise" rather than "perfection." Evolution indicates to people that God chose to relinquish divine power — as in Saint Paul's teaching in Philippians 2, about the divine "self-emptying" — rather than to create a finished universe or to coerce cosmic processes or humans to act in a certain way. The Pauline understanding of a "divine humility" being expressed in the incarnation should be extended to include divine humility being operative during initial and ongoing creation:

> Intrinsic to the divine *kenosis* is authorization of creation's striving for genuine independence vis-à-vis its creator. Love by its very nature cannot compel, and so any God whose very essence is love should not be expected to overwhelm the world either with a coercively directive "power" or an annihilating "presence." Indeed, an infinite love must in some sense "absent" or "restrain itself," precisely in order to give the world the "space" in which to become something distinct from the creative love that constitutes it as "other."[109]

The unfolding of the universe, the evolution of life, and the development of human self-consciousness are all allowed their freedom.

Haught links together evolution, ecology, and eschatology. He declares that an ecological theology consistent with evolutionary processes requires a "metaphysics of the future."[110] This would unite the biblical notion of "promise," and Christian belief in the resurrection of Jesus, to discern "the future fulfillment of the whole universe already made manifest in advance."[111]

John Haught accepts the Christian understanding of a "sacramental nature," but agrees with Thomas Berry that people must also appreciate nature for itself: "And if through faith we can interpret the totality of nature as a great promise, we may learn to treasure it not simply for its sacramental transparency to God but also because it carries in its present perishable glory the seeds of a final, eschatological flowering."[112] Haught wonders whether or not Christians can appreciate the natural world in itself to such an extent that the Christian prayer "Maranatha; Come Lord Jesus" will become "an incentive to love rather than ignore the natural world."[113] People must see nature as *"essentially promise,"* because if it is seen only as a "gift" then it is easily viewed as "something we may consume or use up."[114]

People aware of this potential for human despoliation of nature should seek to "secure the integrity of what evolution has already produced." This does not mean that people should try to preserve a particular stage of evolutionary development, since "the human spirit cannot find fulfillment in any given state of nature" and the renewing Spirit is the "ultimate energy" of the world's evolution; nor does it mean that people should resacralize nature to an extent that is antithetical to the biblical prophets' teaching that people should not have a "suffocating bondage to natural objects and occurrences."[115] Humans must have faith in creation and recognize and respect the worth of all creatures, acknowledging the prospect that "other natural beings have a meaning and value to their creator that may be quite hidden from our human powers of discernment."[116]

In the world of nature there is much "ugliness and unresolved cruelty," but these conditions should not be seen as the last word in the evolutionary process that contains the seeds of eschatological promise. Haught observes that "we do not expect perfection from a promise, but only from its fulfillment."[117] When humans cause ecological devastation, therefore, they harm not only their present historical moment but also "God's own creative envisagement of the future."[118]

In his appreciation for the wonders of nature, and his acceptance of the evolutionary processes initiated by the Creator, Haught suggests—with Thomas Berry and Matthew Fox—that there is an overfocus in Christianity on doctrines of reparation and expiation, which flow from a (now scientifically superseded) understanding of the original humans' fall from their initial state of perfection:

> Evolutionary science, however, has rendered the assumption of an original cosmic perfection, one allegedly debauched by a temporally "original" sin, obsolete and unbelievable. Simultaneously, it has also abolished, at least in principle, the whole cosmological framework in which motifs of reparation and expiation have become so deeply entrenched in our cultures and our classical spiritualities....An often overlooked theological consequence of our new awareness of living in the not-yet-perfected universe that evolution logically implies is that the obsessive repetitiveness of expiation sanctioned by the longing for a lost paradise can no longer plausibly dominate our religious sensibilities.[119]

The ideas of John Haught stimulate reflection in a new direction, toward linking more directly the findings of modern science, theology, and ecological concerns.

The voices from North America have addressed key issues for environmental theology and suggested a rethinking or reinterpretation of some church understandings. They have done so from within the dominant culture, even though they are at times at variance with some of its viewpoints and values. In the South, some of the same issues are addressed, but generally from the perspective of the poor and peoples of color. In that context, ideas about social liberation, including redistribution of property in land and an equitable distribution of the benefits obtained from the land, usually are prioritized above concern for the environment per se.

5
Transforming Tradition and Conserving Creation: Southern Visions

Environmental consciousness emerged not only in North America, but also in Latin America, although with a different initial focus: in the South, land ownership and redistribution have been the major concerns. Poverty of the many, control of the land by a few wealthy landowners, and military dictatorships catalyzed church leaders from the hierarchy, parish clergy, university theologians, and laity to support the poor in their quest for land redistribution. While church documents in the North might speak about a progressive land tax, the South sought redistribution through expropriation (with appropriate compensation to landowners). This idea was reinforced by Pope John Paul II's comments in Cuilapán, Mexico (see chapter 2), when he visited that country to participate in the Puebla Conference of the Latin American Catholic bishops.

Among theologians, the focus on land distribution and economic justice found forceful expression in the writings of theologians of liberation. Over decades, their ideas evolved to an extent: while retaining their passion for justice expressed in ideas about land distribution issues, some adopted a new consciousness of the interdependence of all life and the needs of Earth. As was the case in the preceding chapter, while an individual theologian might change his or her role in the church—which in the South was the choice of Leonardo Boff, for example, who resigned from his priestly status—their ideas might still contribute to developing Catholic environmental theology.

Marcelo de Barros, O.S.B., and José Luis Caravias, S.J.

Throughout Latin America during the last decades of the twentieth century, members of the clergy from several dioceses, along with some bishops, members of religious orders, and lay pastoral workers, became involved in struggles for land for the landless and human rights for indigenous peoples. Marcelo de Barros Souza, a Benedictine priest and monk, and José Luis Caravias, a Jesuit priest, have been among the clergy involved in land issues linked to fundamental human rights. Marcelo de Barros worked with base Christian communities throughout his native Brazil; José Luis Caravias, originally from Spain, served in Latin America for more than forty years, more than twenty-five of which were among indigenous peasants in Ecuador. Their major joint work, *Teología de la Tierra* (in Spanish) and *Teologia da Terra* (in Portuguese), was published in 1988.

Caravias and de Barros note that since the earliest days of the conquest of what eventually became known as the Americas, when Europeans planted their respective flags on shores "that already had millions of inhabitants who were the legitimate owners,"[1] the history of Latin America has been marked by conflicts over land. Currently, with regard to land tenancy, a few people have extensive holdings while the majority of people barely survive. The politics of development imposed by North America result, in South America, in "the enrichment of a minority and the marginalization of the majority."[2] While in the light of faith land "is a gratuitous gift of God, a gift given to all that they might live," in business eyes land is seen in terms of economic profit.[3] Agribusiness takes priority over an agriculture oriented toward the needs of the community. This results in "a lack of food for the people, since the needs of the poor do not count."[4] To this injustice must be added "the ecological destruction that large corporations leave behind after their irrational exploitation of the land."[5] Additionally, land that could be used to benefit the broader community is left undeveloped, despite available technology to extract needed resources, because the large estates use their land solely as a natural prairie or as a speculative financial investment whose profit is lazily awaited. In violation of principles of self-sufficiency, Latin American nations import food instead of using existing lands to produce food, which results in malnutrition for the poor.[6]

In this social context, "few laws exist to protect the small farmers and indigenous peoples; and, frequently, if there are such laws, they are not observed." In order to maintain the violence of these unjust conditions, including an unjust distribution of land, "the violence of arms is needed."[7] Peasant workers who object to these conditions are "persecuted, tortured and murdered," so that eventually they react with violence against their oppression.[8]

Caravias and de Barros criticize transnational capitalism and its practitioner nations' imposition of dependent status on countries of the South: "Their prosperity has been possible thanks to our misery."[9]

Concerning the beliefs and conditions of Latin America's indigenous populations, Caravias and de Barros state that Native peoples respect the land as "Mother Earth," or *Pachamama,* and work with it communally, and do not regard it as merely an object to be used for its instrumental or speculative value. The *indios* regard an attack against their lands as "an attack against their life and their religion." The land is "the foundation upon which community life is sustained."[10] They respect the land's natural rhythms, and adapt to their natural environment and strive to live with it in ecological balance.[11] The authors note that Pope John Paul II affirmed indigenous cultures in his 1985 address in Latacunga, Ecuador: "Since before the time of evangelization there were seeds of Christ in your communities....It was he who enlightened the heart of your peoples, in order that you might discover the footprints of God in all God's creatures: in the sun and in the moon, in the good and great Mother Earth, in the snow and the volcano, in the lagoons and in the rivers that descend from your high mountain ranges."[12] They add to this eloquent language: "We cannot do a theology of the land unless we begin with the vision and the life of the people, especially indigenous people."[13]

Caravias and de Barros analyze rural religious attitudes toward the land, and observe that Amazon region peasants cannot understand how anyone can own the land: someone "can own the fruits of the land, the goods that they obtain from the land, but not the land itself."[14] The traditional rural worker "has an intimate experience of God through their intimate contact with nature....To work God's land is an act of intimate communion with God; it is to collaborate in the work of God, in something that is God's....They see that all creation is good, and that the provident God gives forces and wisdom to make the land produce."[15]

After describing the historical injustices that brought Africans to be slaves in the Americas, the authors advocate a Black theology of the land, because "to do theology of liberation presupposes being situated with the point of view and in the concrete life of the oppressed." They note that a great percentage of the oppressed rural workers are Blacks, direct or mixed-blood descendants of African slaves. Most oppression is white and racist. "From this we can conclude that the theology of the land must include the Black journey, participation and reflection."[16]

Caravias and de Barros hope that the principal fruit of their work is "the liberation of the people and their common possession of the land."[17] From a *theology* of the land flows a *spirituality* of the land, which is "the experience of this road of following Jesus and communion with the God living in the practice of the struggle for the land and of the movement of the rural workers for their liberation and for the divine right they have to live in this land of our continent and to draw from it the sustenance of life."[18] This spirituality presupposes solidarity with the oppressed, and struggling for land with them.[19]

The theology and spirituality of the land are related to hoping in and working for the coming of the reign of God, "uniting a political vision and this faith vision"[20] and seeking greater involvement of women and of the laity in the church's work.[21]

Spirituality is "living the experience of the Spirit of God." In and with this Spirit, people "receive the land as a biblical sacrament of communion with God."[22] (Here, as in later statements by U.S. and Canadian bishops, the sacramental nature of creation is recognized.)

Current policies and practices on the land, and the capitalist ideology that is their foundation, are harmful to the land's productivity and to the well-being of its workers. Alternative ways of thinking and working are needed, since "capitalist agriculture intends to dominate the soil and cultures, doing violence to them," while alternative agricultural practices believe in "a profound interrelation of all the phenomena of nature."[23] In some countries, people who seek an alternative agriculture are discovering "the ancestral techniques of indigenous communities to make fertile and productive lands that are in decline or in altitudes little suited for sowing."[24] Some farmers are using compost and organic fertilizer to clean the land from chemicals and their communities from indebtedness caused by chemical inputs.[25] (In these observations the authors touch, however briefly, upon environmental theology issues beyond the needs of the human community, into the realm of ecological integrity.)

In order to bring about necessary social changes, the poor sometimes resort to violence in order to counteract the ongoing violence of the rich; the context in which they live will determine whether such is their only recourse to overcome oppression. But it should be remembered that "the root of violence in the country is private property."[26] Sometimes unjust conditions are maintained by unjust laws. Rural workers have learned that "not everything that is legal is just." And when unjust laws and social

structures are kept in place by force of arms, a land ministry recognizes that peasants have a "sacred right" to defend themselves
and their families.[27] In doing so they must remember to "love their
enemy."[28] (DeBarros and Caravias here accept revolutionary violence as sometimes necessary, for defensive reasons. Their perspective contrasts with that of the bishops of the Dominican
Republic, seen in chapter 2, who oppose peasants' use of violence
or of land occupations to achieve justice.)

In a presentation at the "Theology of the Land" conference
in Itatiaia, Brazil, after the publication of their book, Marcelo de
Barros spoke about "Land Ministry and the Challenge of Spirituality." He noted again that the reign of God was a basic element of
the theology of the land, that in fact land ministry "was presented
as an announcement and prophecy of the Reign of God."[29] He
elaborated further that "since the God in whom we believe is the
Lord of justice, the God of life, which is revealed in God's reign,
our spirituality is and must always be of justice and of hope, that
is, of the Reign of God." He sees in the suffering and martyrdom
of rural workers a "high point of spirituality," an almost "mystical
experience of suffering." He declares further that "living the
memory of the martyrs, the denunciations of injustices and the
hope for liberation of the land, we are contemplating in the midst
of all this the Lord, the living God," who is walking with the least
of the people.[30] De Barros closes noting the necessity of "living
fully this communion of the land, as a sacrament of God."[31]

Marcelo de Barros and José Luis Caravias develop their theology of the land and their spirituality of the land primarily from
the point of view of landless peasants living amid an abundance
of land owned by the wealthy few. The peasants must work the
land for another's profit rather than their own or to meet their
needs. The owners leave some of their land idle, despite the peasants' needs, holding it solely for its speculative value or as a status
symbol. From the perspective of the landless poor, de Barros and
Caravias support the immediate need for social justice, and do not
consider the plight of other members of the biotic community or

the integrity of ecosystems. The desperate situation of the oppressed human community overwhelms consideration of broader issues. Their allusions to alternative agriculture and the sacramental nature of the land, however, are seeds for a future development of their thought to include environmental considerations beyond agricultural land ownership and use.

Leonardo Boff

The writings of Leonardo Boff link the groans of Earth and the cries of the poor for liberation. In much of the twentieth century, as just seen, community leaders and theologians in Latin America were particularly preoccupied with issues of economic injustice, including the inequitable distribution of land. "Earth issues" were essentially issues of redistributing land to the oppressed poor and ensuring that the poor had at least the necessities of life, which are derived from the goods of the land. The statement of the Mexican revolutionary Emiliano Zapata earlier in the twentieth century has been extensively quoted not only in his native land but also throughout Latin America: "The land belongs to everyone, like the water, the air, and the light and warmth of the sun. And those who work the land with their own hands have a right to it."

In Boff's native Brazil, the Catholic Church became involved with the struggles of the landless farmers, many of whom had been forced from their lands. Clergy worked with laity in organizing demonstrations and in occupying unused land to try to build communities and grow food. Several people were killed in the process, but some lands eventually were redistributed from the rich to the poor. In theological writings from that social context, land redistribution is a paramount issue. Environmental consciousness and a sense of Earth-based spirituality are absent, or are only hinted at. Leonardo Boff wrote at first in a similar vein, but then as his ecological consciousness emerged, linked to his heritage as a Franciscan priest, he began to relate economic justice and ecojustice. His first work discussing this relationship was *Ecology and Liberation: A New Paradigm.*

Boff affirms from the beginning of his book the interrelatedness of all being. He declares that "everything that exists, co-exists" and is part of an "infinite web of all-inclusive relations."[32] These ideas help to bring ecological issues into consideration in Latin America.

Boff observes that the "population of the world is growing at an alarming rate"[33] and wonders, "Will the earth's ecosystem be able to sustain so many people?"[34] (In raising the population issue in this way, Boff departs from the stance of representatives of the South who reject population concerns as a northern perspective, and suggest that First World consumption, not Third World population, is the major cause of environmental degradation.)

Boff's thought developed within the theology of liberation perspective, and he links that with the environmental crises confronting the Earth. He states that the poor are forced to exhaust needed resources out of necessity, unable to conserve for the future because of their desperate struggle for survival, while the rich waste resources to satisfy their wants. So, Boff declares, "It is as important to contribute to the reproduction of nature as to ensure that the interests of the work force are safeguarded," and he observes approvingly that C. S. Lewis stated that human power over nature is really the "power exercised by some people over others, using nature as a tool." He adds that "social injustice leads to ecological injustice, and vice-versa."[35] The present dominant social model is "a social sin (the rupture of social relations) and an ecological sin (the rupture of relations between humankind and the environment)."[36]

Along with other contemporary theologians, Boff asserts that "rights" cannot be limited exclusively to human individuals and groups: "Rights do not belong only to humankind and to nations, but also to other beings in creation. There is a human and social right, but there is also an ecological and cosmic right. We do not have the right to what we have not created."[37] In his later work, *Cry of the Earth, Cry of the Poor,* he observes that "all things in nature are citizens, have rights, and deserve respect and reverence....Today, the common good is not exclusively human; it is the common good of all nature."[38] He believes that a "biotic democracy" is needed, that "we must move toward a planetary ecological and social democracy."[39] People must practice generational solidarity: "Future generations have the right to inherit a conserved earth and a healthy biosphere."[40]

Boff declares, as do traditional theology and diverse peoples in their descriptions of spiritual experience, that God leaves signs of divine presence in creation. God speaks to people through creatures, since "every creature is a messenger of God, and God's representative as well as sacrament."[41] The creatures as sacraments manifest the immanence of the Creator in creation, witnessing to "the reality of the Spirit's indwelling in creation. The Spirit has made the cosmos a temple, the scene of the Spirit's action and manifestation." This understanding is not pantheistic, but pan*en*theistic: "Not everything is God, but God is in everything....God flows through all things; God is present in everything and makes of all reality a temple....The world is not only a bridge to God. It is also the place where God is honored and worshiped, and the place where we meet God."[42]

The perception of signs of God in creation is not limited to members of a particular religion, nor is any one religion the only path to God. Rather, "so that we may one day experience the Mystery that we call God, everything is a way and all living creatures are sacraments and gates to a meeting with God."[43] Therefore, "the Spirit is not imprisoned in religious institutions."[44] Boff asserts that faith is based on individual experience, and needs to be internalized and responded to—personally and communally. Then, "faith is the expression of an encounter with God which embraces all existence and feeling—the heart, the intellect, and the will. The occasions and times of such encounters become sacraments, points of reference to a form of experience that is overwhelmingly, irrefutably significant." From this experience emerges theology, which represents "an attempt to translate a fundamental experience into terms proper to reason (doctrine), practice (ethics), and celebration (liturgy)."[45]

In *Cry of the Earth, Cry of the Poor,* Leonardo Boff develops further his themes of liberation for Earth and for peoples of Earth. He states at the outset that "the aim of this book is to connect the cry of the oppressed with the cry of the Earth," and he laments that "humans have shown that they can commit not only homicide and ethnocide, but biocide and geocide as well."[46] In the current state of things, the poor are the "most threatened of God's creatures."[47] Because of these connections between environmental devastation and human oppression, "ecological justice has to go hand in hand with social justice."[48] The two are thoroughly intertwined: "Social (in)justice cannot be separated from ecological (in)justice."[49]

Boff acknowledges that the human intellect has developed science and technology beneficial for people—but also harmful to them and to the Earth. The time has come to use science and technology *for* Nature, not *against* Nature.[50]

Reflecting modern scientific understandings, Boff speaks about the universe's *autopoiesis,* its self-organizing capability, as an ongoing cosmogenesis, the way in which God chooses to create.[51] Within and because of cosmogenesis, "everything is spiritual" and "all things are related."[52]

It is necessary to reclaim the sacred to begin a new covenant with the Earth. Otherwise, "ecology will become merely a technique for managing human voracity but never for overcoming it."[53] People need to develop an intimate association with the Earth, because "only a personal relationship with Earth makes us love it. We do not exploit but respect and reverence the one we love."[54]

Commenting on the idea of a "fall" from grace and cosmic punishment, Boff declares that "the idea that the Earth with all that exists and moves on it must be punished because of human sin denotes a limitless anthropocentrism."[55] He believes that "Paradise is a prophecy of the future projected back upon the past";[56]

earthly paradise is a promise of the future, not a nostalgia for the past.[57] He sees Jesus as the "definitive being"[58] of creation, and declares that because of God's desire for self-communion with creation "the Incarnation of the Son was not due to human sin….The Son would have been incarnated regardless of sin."[59] Jesus Christ "was the preexisting Word, he became the incarnate Word, and finally he has become the transfigured Word."[60] The "reign of God" taught by Jesus symbolizes "the gradual realization of God's project for all creation."[61]

Boff declares of humans, "We are sons and daughters of Earth, we are the Earth itself become self-aware….When an ecological agronomist studies soil composition, the cosmos is studying itself. When an astronomer points a telescope toward the stars, the universe is gazing at itself." The universe and the Earth see themselves through the human observer.[62] It is not enough, however, merely to study the universe; it is necessary to experience them deeply.[63] People might realize then that "human beings were created for the universe—not vice versa."[64]

The universe comes from a Creator who existed before the Big Bang, permeates and continually creates the world, and is immanent in the world, transparent through it, and transcendent to it.[65] Therefore, "creation thus understood is a vast book written internally and externally that bears God's signature: 'Deo creato, made by God.'…[It] contains God's ongoing revelation and is the most deep-rooted and continuous manifestation of the sacred."[66]

Leonardo Boff offers insightful links between liberation theology and environmental theology. His prior commitment to the poor is retained and integrated with his overall communion with creation as a whole.

Ivone Gebara

Ivone Gebara, a Brazilian Sister of Our Lady (Canoneses of Saint Augustine), presents an ecofeminist liberation perspective from an urban Brazilian social context. She believes that the major ecological, economic, and ecclesial problems and injustices present today are the result of patriarchy permeating social systems. In speaking about her personal engagement with the Earth, Gebara exclaimed, "I feel such a great passion for the world!" and added that "it strengthens me to see myself as part of this earth, neither more nor less, but part of it. I am seed, daughter, fruit, earth. This earth is my soul and my body." She lamented the church's unwillingness to dialogue, declaring that "the institutional church, not the church as the people of God, but the hierarchical church, is afraid of the world." She expressed the hope that human beings around the world would join hands "wanting to create a new face of humanity, a new and different world!"[67]

Gebara seeks to develop an ecofeminist and ecumenical ecological theology oriented toward eliminating oppression of the poor and of the Earth by the politically, religiously, and economically powerful. Her insights on patriarchy in church and society offer a powerful analysis of the use of religious language to maintain the dual and linked oppression of women and the Earth. Her major work on these themes is *Longing for Running Water: Ecofeminism and Liberation.*

Gebara acknowledges from the beginning "the poverty of my experience with the world of nature and of animals!" but declares that while she remains "an urban woman" she now has a "different perception of things—a bodily perception of the unity and interdependence of all living things and a growing awareness that we are one body with the whole universe."[68] She says that she is developing, from her experience particularly as a church worker with the urban poor, "an urban ecofeminism." She hopes to see the birth of "a future that promises deeper communion between human beings and all other living things."[69] She is concerned for and passionate about "the struggle for survival in which innumerable people in my country, especially women and children, continue to be immersed."[70] She notes that the cleanliness and better appearance of rich people's neighborhoods does not result from the work of the rich but of the poor, usually women. This is "the logic of the capitalist system, with its narrow exclusiveness, as well as the logic of hierarchical patriarchy and of class, race, and gender privilege."[71]

The poor, who suffer most of the consequences of ecological devastation, are not the causes of it and benefit little from it. While Gebara does not use the terms *eco-racism* and *eco-classism,* such are the ideologies and practices that she describes as devastating to the life of the poor. She observes that the poor do not produce most of the waste, nor do they own nuclear power plants, plan wars, or consume most canned and packaged goods—but they are the first to be harmed by the wastes produced by others.[72]

Gebara notes a major difference in environmental approaches in the North and South, based on their different experiences. While people in the North focus on saving Earth and its rivers and forests, peoples in the South seek to learn to live on the land and build homes on it, and strive to effect rural land reform and to redistribute urban lots.[73]

Gebara laments that even in liberation theologies emerging from Latin America, there has been little discussion of feminist or ecological issues. This is because of the patriarchal, hierarchical church structure; even theologians talking about social and eco-logical change are limited in their ideas and writings by patriarchal concepts—theological and political—contained in the language they employ, because people within the church "fail to see that we often formulate our protests from within this same hierarchical power system, without altering our understanding of the human person, of God, and of Jesus."[74] She wonders whether alternative theological thought can emerge, since "our church institutions have always tended to absolutize their patriarchal forms of thought and organization, as if they were 'revealed by God.'"[75]

The anthropocentrism that is a part of us as humans "needs to be complemented by a wider biocentrism, an acknowledgment of the central importance of all life-forms." People cannot detach their human reality from their "wider cosmic identity."[76] People are not in an isolated human context; they are interdependent in and related to the rest of nature. People do not recognize the importance of their interdependence, but if they were to do so, with an ecofeminist perspective, they would "be able to care for the earth and all its inhabitants as if they were close relatives, as parts of our greater body, without which individual life and con-sciousness are impossible.…We need to introduce the notion of communication with, rather than conquest of, the earth and space."[77] For Gebara, nature and culture are not exclusive, but are "interconnected components that allow us to be what we are and allow the earth to be what it is today."[78]

In regard to the role of people in the cosmos, Gebara states that "the human 'person' [is] the subject/object that is able to reflect on itself and to be the thinking dimension of the universe." As such, people are to work for justice and mercy in cultural sys-tems. In her enthusiasm to change oppressive social conditions, Gebara states, "To reflect on the meaning of the human person is to accept the challenge of becoming creators of ourselves *and of the entire living world"* (emphasis added).[79] (This anthropocentric attitude that humans are creators of the whole biotic community is uncharacteristic of Gebara, and modifies and conflicts with her declaration elsewhere that humans with all beings are part of a sacred body.)

Gebara critiques statements about human origins and the human role in creation that are expressed in the *Catechism of the Catholic Church*. She notes that §374 of the *Catechism* declares that the "first man" was created good and lived in harmony with all creation in a "state that would be surpassed only by the glory of the new creation in Christ."[80] Gebara would rather affirm, in the light of scientific understandings, "the mysterious origin of the cosmos, of all beings, and of humanity itself," by recognizing that there was no original idyllic state with ethical perfection that was interrupted by evil.[81] Gebara adds that "to acknowledge the mysterious origin of all beings is to affirm their freedom in the vital process of evolution itself,"[82] an observation that resonates with the ideas of *kenosis* expressed by John Haught. She states further that "we can no longer be the center by means of which all is dominated. Rather, we have to be the center through which all enters into fraternal communion."[83]

Gebara further criticizes the *Catechism* because it expresses "an absolute discontinuity between the Creator God and all of creation." The *Catechism* teaches "a hierarchical understanding of the world, one that is not necessarily Christian." This understanding justifies male, ethnic, religious, and class domination, which are destructive of peoples and Earth.[84]

Gebara advocates a collective understanding of *person* that is not only anthropological but "cosmic," and characterized by "relatedness." She describes relatedness as "the primary reality" that is "constitutive of all beings."[85] The experience of relatedness can have practical consequences, stimulating people's consciousness of "a dimension of ecojustice in which the life of other beings is essential to the living out of human justice. Ecojustice is the kind of justice we seek and live out when we affirm our bodies as part of the Sacred Body of the universe."[86]

Ivone Gebara links justice for people with justice for the Earth in a way parallel to Leonardo Boff, but adds dimensions of urban life and the perspective of ecofeminism. She affirms "the engagement of ecofeminism in struggles for social justice, and, beyond that, in the struggle for eco-justice, which requires a wider and more global perspective."[87] She states that believers need to replace an "anthropocentric Christianity" with "a more biocentric understanding of salvation. To Jesus' humanistic perspective, we need to add an ecological perspective."[88]

When perspectives from North and South are compared, several differences emerge as well as some similarities. In the North, capitalism is usually taken as a given, the needs of the poor are addressed sparingly, and the environment in itself is a focus; in the South, capitalism is an instrument of oppression of the people, the needs of the poor are paramount, and the environment has generally been viewed as the context for resources to meet the needs of the oppressed. In both hemispheres, the sacramentality of nature is affirmed, as is intergenerational responsibility.

The perspectives presented by the preceding visionaries of both North and South "stretch the envelope" of the relationship of theology and ecology, much the same as did the ideas of Teilhard de Chardin (1881–1955) in the area of the relationship of theology to science. Some of Teilhard's understandings became influential in the deliberations and documents of Vatican II, and in church developments since. In a complementary way, many of the ideas just presented, after they have been critically analyzed over time, might very well find themselves incorporated into church teachings. The process of a transition in the Catholic environmental tradition, from the dominion attitude to a more relational consciousness, should continue, in any case, in the decades to come. The possibilities for a transformation in environmental practices would be enhanced if the latter were to happen. Should this occur, Christians would find themselves to a certain extent where their ancestors were millennia ago: appreciating the immanence of the Creator in creation, and understanding the intrinsic sacredness of creation. A significant difference from those ancient attitudes that were the foundation of religious thinking is that scientific discoveries have brought additional knowledge and responsibilities. In contemporary environmental theology, an enhanced appreciation of the complex processes underlying the cosmic dance adds a deeper dimension of awe as humans stand in wonder and humility before the grandeur of the universe. The ideas advanced to date, and those yet to be developed, will continue to build upon the core Catholic tradition and to transform it.

6
Creation Consciousness and Concern

The Earth's environmental crisis—which in reality is a crisis of human consciousness and morally responsible activity—has led to renewed reflection on the place and role of humanity in the cosmos. Initially, as seen earlier, Catholic Church teachings recalled ideas and an ideology from centuries ago: a dominion perspective in which humans were at the top of a pyramid. All other creatures, indeed all creation, support humanity and were intended for human use. More recent teachings—that Earth as property in land must be equitably shared, and that the goods of Earth must be responsibly distributed—have become part of that older tradition. But anthropocentrism continued: "man" was still to exercise dominion, but was to share the fruits of that dominion with other "men."

As the ranks of theologians became augmented by increasing numbers of the laity, and as they and members of religious orders and the clergy—priests and bishops—became more engaged with the concrete problems facing Earth and all creatures, a gradual transformation in church understandings began to develop. While not all of the new perspectives were accepted, and while some of those that were accepted were not incorporated into church teachings in their entirety, new insights and new practices began to become part of the ecological consciousness of Catholicism.

The most significant developments in Catholic environmental thought, as expressed in the most recent church documents, were seven:

1. The use of the term *sacramental universe,* with a complementary renewed celebration of the immanence of God in creation
2. The teaching that care for creation is an essential part of what it means to be a Christian
3. The understanding that regional or bioregional assessments of environmental issues are needed, and that means for addressing them must be devised
4. A developing sense of the sacredness and dignity of all creation
5. A recognition of the relationship between environmental degradation and human poverty
6. The emerging shift from decidedly anthropocentric-dominion ideas to a stewardship-caretaking perspective, and
7. The beginning of a subtle shift from the stewardship perspective to a relational consciousness in church teachings about humanity's interdependence with other creatures, in their common and integrated ecosystems, within creation as a whole.

Several of these developments require further elaboration here, and continuing exploration not only in environmental theology, but in the more philosophically based traditional systematic theology as well. Issues that complement the teachings just mentioned are presented briefly; these are seeds for further growth in the fertile soil of a dynamic theology rich in tradition, nourished by living water, and open to the loving breath of the Spirit.

God Transcendent and Immanent

Christianity at times has viewed the Earth as being solely the locus for human salvific striving; understood the kingdom of God as being solely "up in heaven" or beyond and unrelated to that Earth locus; and seen God as being solely transcendent, essentially detached from an engaged relationship with humanity and the rest of creation. Such attitudes contrast starkly with creation-affirming teachings that emerge from a careful consideration of the implications of God's incarnation in Jesus, the content and implications of the Lord's Prayer, and the resurrection of Jesus. All of these affirm the goodness of the corporeal reality of human existence. A key perception of theology in conversation with environmental issues is that God is both *transcendent*—distinct from the created world—and *immanent*—present to the world: in God the world "lives and moves and has its being." Environmental concern—care for creation, in Christian thought—has heightened human consciousness of the immanence of the Creator in creation, including the belief that this divine presence is seen in a unique way in Jesus.

Within this context, an exclusive focus on God-transcendent is being modified to include an appreciation of God-immanent. The latter understanding is more in accord with the personal relationship with God advocated by Jesus: God is "Abba," which is an intimate and affectionate designation of God as "Dad," a closeness not appreciated in the more formal "Father."

But the sense of God-immanent is not to be limited solely to human–divine personal engagement. It extends across and deep within creation. The Spirit permeates all of creation; all creation in some way has the potential to be revelatory of divine presence. On such occasions, this experience of divine presence is a sacramental moment in the sacramental commons of a sacramental universe.

The Center: Creator and Creation

A particular issue that comes to the fore in considerations about creation is the place of humans in the cosmos. Traditional cultural perceptions in the geographic areas where Christianity was born and first developed were that the Earth was the center of the universe and humankind was at the center of a creation created to serve the human species. The scientific discoveries of Copernicus and Galileo ideologically displaced the Earth's position; the theories of Darwin began to alter the human position; and perceptions from traditional indigenous spirituality and a developing Christian theology are suggesting that "image of God" means more a caring relationship *with* all creatures rather than a superordinate position *over* all creatures, and an integration into an evolving and complex universe, the wonders of which humans are only beginning to perceive and appreciate, and before which they might now stand in humility and awe. Human pride of place can give way to humility of position, in a context of awe before the grandeur of creation that leads people to appreciate the creativity and power of God. The "images" become aware of God's solicitous care for all creation and their responsibility to act in like manner. Human consciousness, when open to and engaged with God the Creator, apprehends more of the heights and depths of creation itself, accepts a relational role with all creatures, and assumes responsibility to care for those parts of creation entrusted to human care. These ideas are difficult for many to accept, because they de-center the human species. But the ideas offer an opportunity for people to become open to God's intentions for humanity rather than to continue humanity's appropriation of a perceived divine justification for theoretical anthropocentrism in, and practical domination of, God's creation.

The new human perspective might be termed a *creatiocentric consciousness*. A creation-centered consciousness is not theocentric, geocentric, or biocentric. In essence, it is all of these, since "creation" indicates both a Creator and the concretization of divine creativity in creatures and in a creative process. In creation, divine vision is realized: it is both "becoming real" (a dynamic process, such as evolution) and "become real" (a final product, such as the basic operative laws of the universe discerned through the study of physics, chemistry, and biology).

In the *theo*centric aspect of creation-centered consciousness, humans recognize their role as the creatures with whom the Creator is most engaged rationally, who are potentially the self-conscious reflection of creation as a whole and are thereby creation's ongoing dialogue partner with the Creator, and who because of all of these intricacies of human existence have the most responsibility in creation. In the *geo*centric aspect of a creation-centered consciousness, humankind acknowledges its need to respect the being and rhythms of Earth and to adapt itself to these as much as possible rather than solely to adapt Earth to itself. People might alter Earth's terrain and Earth's goods to meet human needs and satisfy human wants, but they must come to recognize their ultimate dependence on the nurturing well-being of Earth and alter their own policies and practices to ensure its continuance. At this moment humanity sees Earth as home and, in the words of Francis of Assisi, as Sister and Mother, both a fellow creature and the primary provider of the elemental conditions and material goods needed for human existence. In the *bio*centric aspect of creation-centered consciousness, people recognize that they are interrelated, interdependent, and integrated members of the community of all life. The relational component of human life in this community requires additional consideration.

Toward a Relational Consciousness

Christians historically have perceived humankind's role in creation to be a divinely appointed domination or dominion over, stewardship of, or relation with other creatures. Theology is in a still-unfolding development of perspectives in this area: from a human monarchic superiority over creation to human integration with creation.

In this issue, Indian peoples of the Americas present for consideration and incorporation elements of their traditional spirituality. The planet on which the community of life lives is Mother Earth; all creatures on Mother Earth are respected and are regarded as relatives: traditional elders in some traditions, for example, open rituals or meetings with the phrase "Greetings, all my relations," in which the "relations" are not just humans but all living creatures. The greeting sometimes is made more explicit: "Greetings to all the two-legged people, all the four-legged people, all the winged people, all the finned people, all the rooted people." A profound sense of relatedness is obvious here, reminiscent of Francis of Assisi's designation of all members of creation, living and nonliving, as "brother" and "sister."

A relational consciousness makes people aware of the beauty and vitality of all of the natural world of which they are a part. It stimulates a greater appreciation of all of nature, a sense of kinship with all life, and an awareness of the divine sparks and individual spirits in other creatures. This consciousness stimulates a mystical bonding with creatures in themselves, and can also lead beyond them to the Spirit immanent within and permeating all creation.

Co-evolutionary Processes

The universe, in Catholic thought, is still being created. God's creative work did not end after six "days" of creation, whether these are seen as each lasting twenty-four hours or billions of years. Creation, the Catholic Catechism says, is in statu viae, a state of development; it is an ongoing work. The dynamics of the physical universe are paralleled by evolution in the biological dimension of existence and also, in Christian thought, by evolution of the reign of God in human history. These three are complementary and inextricably interwoven evolutionary processes. The universe expands and brings forth new combinations of elements and energy; the biotic community diversifies and complexifies on Earth and perhaps, as new scientific discoveries reveal, on other planets in this solar system and in other solar systems as yet unknown; and humanity makes periodic progress, although with aberrant steps backward on occasion, toward fulfillment of the Lord's Prayer that God's "will be done on Earth as it is in heaven."

To the three preceding co-evolutionary processes might be added a fourth: theology in dynamic engagement with the first three. In all the processes, whether physical, biological, social, or intellectual, there is a core in each dimension that remains constant while transformations and iterations take place on its outer edge and sometimes flow toward or become part of the center. Science discovers the basic laws underlying the constants and contingents of the cosmos, and uses working hypotheses or theories to seek further data and knowledge; theology discovers basic truths at the foundation of the creative process, and uses intuitive and speculative thought (and sometimes mystical experience) to understand better both divine Being and divine engagement with creation, subjecting that thought to the test of both time and competing proposals from within the Christian tradition (and beyond, since God does not confine divine communication solely to one religion, or one culture, or one ethnic group, or one era). Indeed, as Catholic bishops have pointed out, the entire universe is sacramental, revelatory of God to the person of faith and to the person open to faith; and, as biblical theology has taught, God is revealed in divine acts in human history. The caution of the prophet Amos to ancient Israel is relevant today as a corrective to religious or ethnic or nationalistic exclusivity: "'Are you not like the Ethiopians to me, O men of Israel?' says the Lord. 'Did I not bring the Israelites from the land of Egypt as I brought the Philistines from Caphtor and the Arameans from Kir?'" (9:7).

Humans once began speculating about the presence of a greater Spirit by observing the wonders of the universe before whose grandeur they stood in awe. Over time, religious institutions became less creation-based and more culture-based, and developed doctrines about divine presence, being and laws based more on cultural understandings of reality and on abstract speculations about God; the latter often were founded in prior human intellectual constructs regarding the divine, and limited by the constraints on human life and thought of particular cultures, places, and historical eras. In the theological co-evolutionary process, peoples of faith who departed historically from their earlier creation-related perspective are reappropriating it, while using new theological and scientific understandings to deepen it beyond earlier and simpler understandings of the natural world, and earlier limited and constraining beliefs about the spiritual dimension of reality.

Human Evil and Natural Catastrophes in Creation

The affirmations that God calls all creation "good" and is solicitous about creatures are confronted on occasion—sometimes quite dramatically—by events harmful to humans and to other members of the biotic community. Wars, terrorism, torture, and political and economic oppression afflict human communities across the world, where people harm people; earthquakes, tornadoes, hurricanes, floods, and volcanic eruptions alter the landscape and kill, hurt, and dislocate people and other living beings with natural disasters. In the first instance, human evil is expressed; in the second, natural catastrophes take their toll. In both cases, people ask how a knowing, good, and powerful Spirit could allow such events to happen: Why did God not intervene on the side of good people suffering from evil human acts? Why did God not prevent the storm that took so many young lives, or answer the prayers of parents whose child was dying of some incurable disease? Why did God create a world with such suffering, and why is death the eventual lot of all life?

Recent responses to such questions from within the Christian tradition try to come to terms with the human condition and situation in an evolutionary cosmos. The universe as a whole is known to be dynamic; life on Earth is evolving; God is creative and good, and not only is concerned about those who suffer, but suffers with them. The integration of three fundamental concepts helps to provide some response to the human anguish represented by the questions people raise. These concepts are process, freedom, and *kenosis*.

The universe is in the process of journeying toward the fulfillment of divine envisioning. Stars are born and disappear in incomprehensible explosions; species emerge, evolve, and become extinct. Some stars continue burning, new stars are born; some species continue evolving, new species emerge. All of creation is part of this process, which results from the power of the existing and developing natural laws operative in the cosmos, and from chance events resulting from the interaction of those laws. Humans have emerged as the most complex organisms known within the created and creating process.

A fundamental characteristic of divine being is freedom. The Creator Spirit values this attribute to such a degree, and simultaneously cares for creation to such an extent, that the Spirit has granted freedom to the universe in whole and in part.

The loving Spirit does not will that creatures suffer, but does will that creatures have freedom to make their own choices, some of which will conflict with choices made by others in the geophysical, ecological, or social areas of their existence. In order to allow this freedom to operate, the Spirit voluntarily refrains from coercing the cosmos or communities of the cosmos by a commanding or otherwise overpowering presence. This cosmic *kenosis,* a self-emptying of divine power, is exemplified in the Christian tradition not only in the evolutionary processes evident to everyone, but in the incarnation evident to the eyes of faith. As Paul so eloquently states in his letter to the Philippians, Christ Jesus, "though he was in the form of God, did not regard equality with God something to be grasped, rather, he emptied himself, taking the form of a slave, coming in human likeness" even to the extent of enduring death by crucifixion (2:6–8). The *kenosis* of Christ Jesus might be regarded as a second divine divestiture of power, the first having occurred as the universe began to emerge from the vision and creative power of God, and continuing thereafter. And just as the Creator grants freedom to the cosmos so, too, Jesus does not coerce but invites people to be his followers: "Come, follow me."

Death is the means of transition from a primarily material mode of being engaged with physical realities while occasionally consciously relating to a spiritual dimension, to a multidimensional but primarily spiritual mode of being engaged with the totality of reality. Death enables the evolution of species to continue, with beneficial complexification and diversification of life, and it permits the passage of generations within a species so that it might go on existing in the niches appropriate to it; death enables new life and new descendants to find room on and needed goods from Earth. These practical benefits of death in an evolutionary world might be small comfort to those with no hope for an afterlife, except as they accept biological analyses of the necessity of death in order that life might benefit, and that their own descendants (or descendants of other members of the human species) might experience the evolving human spiritual, social, and corporeal way of being. For people with a faith perspective, the question might remain as to why the Creator would allow life to end with seeming finality. A reply to that question in this life and at this historical moment in the evolution of human life, intellect, and consciousness might be that in order to realize the divine vision, the Creator chose the best cosmic process possible for that to happen, a process operating freely with elements of necessity, contingency, time, and transition. (The latter cosmic condition is the replacement or displacement of prior generations or types of beings, a "rite of passage" permeating cosmic existence and dynamics, a characteristic of a universe in a constant state of being-becoming as necessity-contingency-time interrelate.)

On occasion, the Spirit might choose to exercise divine freedom as a corrective measure when a competing cosmic freedom or human freedom causes the universe or humanity to stray from the path and from the state that would enable it to reach its highest physical, social, and spiritual potential. The Spirit in its being-becoming, while permeating and engaged with the dynamics of the universe and biotic evolution, does not entirely exercise *kenosis*. The Spirit is still free, and the Spirit who is love and who suffers with the suffering (including, in Christian doctrine, as exemplified in Jesus on the cross) can choose to use creatively the very laws of the universe, in ways anticipating their future interactions, to ameliorate suffering or otherwise to guide or assist the realization of divine vision. A static condition of divine *kenosis* eternally exercised vis-à-vis creation would reduce the Creator Spirit to a variation of the divine watchmaker who casts away creation and remains detached from it: to this medieval understanding would be added the new belief that the watchmaker is voluntarily detached from creation to allow it freedom, and is suffering with creation when that freedom enables biotic suffering and death in the long journey to cosmic and biotic fulfillment. A universal and absolute divine granting of and participation in *process* would reduce the Creator Spirit to an ineffectual observer who is part of what is observed, and who experiences its struggles and sufferings, but is unable to share in its freedom while being so strongly engaged with it. A universal and frequent exercise of divine *intervention,* whether as a "god of the gaps" or as a *deus ex machina,* would eliminate cosmic and biotic freedom during the Spirit's active engagement with love or the Spirit's arbitrary exercise of controlling power. The free and loving Spirit must have, even in creation, the ability to act over cosmic time in those occasional places and situations where love, the greatest of divine attributes, impels the Spirit to override both *kenosis* and human freedom. Otherwise, the Spirit would be reduced to being in a state subordinate to, or, at most, equivalent to, the highest level of the freedom exercised in creation. The question still remains, then, why such divine interventions are only occasional; a response might be that such is required by a balance of love and freedom, and a balance of divine vision and cosmic action, in the ongoing cosmic dance of Creator and creation: to meet an exceptional need, to respond to the human reflective consciousness that acknowledges the Creator Spirit and is engaged in humble petitioning conversation with this divine being, or to compassionately provide needed help out of mercy even when unsolicited, all of this done ultimately and lovingly to guide the universe, and the biotic community within it, toward the best of what it can be, its attainment of its omega state, and its fulfillment of divine hope, expectation, and vision.

The Spirit suffers with those who suffer and engages with creatures in anticipation of future states of being-becoming. In this condition, the Spirit can choose to exercise love: not by violating cosmic laws that the Spirit has initiated and allowed to unfold, but in anticipation of what will eventually emerge from their interaction with each other and with chance events. Perhaps parallel to a theoretical mathematician who builds upon existing knowledge and is able to project next stages, the creative divine mind calculates what is possible from specific interactions at some future time, and draws upon that insight and from divine power to act with loving guidance and compassion in the present. There is here a kind of *anticipatory anamnesis:* not a recall of things past, a transcending of time to make the past present to participate in it in this moment, but a prescient participation in things future, a retrojection of what would eventually be possible in future times and places if necessity, contingency, time, and transition continued to form that future, transcending time to make the future present, a *precall* of what will be or can be; it is a precalling of the future to the present and a present participation in the future, effected by a loving act done not to control or obviate cosmic and biotic freedom, but ultimately to better enable it and enhance it. Such an *anticipatory anamnesis* is a divine contingent act: just as chance events intervene in apparent cosmic regularity, divine action alters a situation or a direction into new and unforeseen possibilities or states of being-becoming; thus, divine intervention does not "violate" freedom or physical, chemical, or biological laws, but is a comparable contingency impacting the necessity of these laws. The divine intellect, integrating the actualities and potentialities of laws and projecting the possibilities of contingent influences upon them, understands possible new combinations; in extraordinary circumstances the Spirit uses this knowledge of the possible future to make it part of the existing present, lovingly to bring a development—that would or might have occurred in the future—back into the present to effect a good. Love, the essence of Spirit, is prioritized over freedom, an attribute of the Creator Spirit that is granted to creation. In this regard, Paul's teaching about *kenosis* (Phil 2:6–7), a description of divine and cosmic freedom, is complemented by Paul's teaching that love is the greatest virtue (1 Cor 13:13), by Jesus' teaching that love is the Greatest Commandment (Matt 22:37–40), and by John's teaching that "God is love" (1 John 4:16).

The current state of reflection on human evil and natural catastrophes in creation is not exhausted in this brief glimpse of some speculations from theology. But the ideas just expressed do give some indication how findings from the physical sciences might prove ultimately to be helpful to theology in reconciling problems of evil and disasters in the world with the existence of a creative and loving Spirit.

Commitment to Creation and to the Preferential Option for the Poor

Catholic Church theologians and members of the hierarchy, including the pope, have called repeatedly for a "preferential option for the poor" (a phrase first used by the Latin American bishops in their "Puebla Document") to be implemented in

church teaching and practice. The church also has declared that
care for creation is an "essential" part of Christian faith and practice. How do Christians conserve their environment and relate to
all members of the broader biotic community when there are so
many poor people on Earth?

In the Catholic tradition, a foundational teaching has been
that God intends that the Earth's goods provide for the basic
needs of humanity. Ideally, distributive justice would ensure that
everyone's need (but not everyone's greed) would be met, in
property, in land, and in basic food, clothing, shelter, energy, and
medicine. When the environment is devastated by adverse human
practices (such as dumping harmful effluents into rivers, releas-
ing harmful emissions into the air, and pouring chemical wastes
onto the land), the needs of the entire human family cannot be
met. If people care for the environment, Earth will be able to produce what humanity needs. The practice of reserving arable lands
from production and retaining them solely for their speculative
value also promotes environmental harm, as desperate poor and
hungry people try to make marginal lands productive. If land and
wealth were distributed equitably, this would not occur. Finally,
goods produced must be distributed equitably, with the first concern being to provide for people's needs. There is probably sufficient food production today to prevent hunger, but food does not
reach those most in need of it. Distribution must be accompanied
by *re*distribution so that those with advantages of wealth and
property in the present will not carry these into the future.

Commitment to creation means concern for the biotic community and the human community that are part of creation. Environmental restoration and conservation will enable ecosystems to thrive
and the needs of all to be met within their natural life cycles.

Environmental Racism

One environmental issue generally missing from both official Catholic statements and the works of individual theologians

of both North and South is eco-racism: environmental injustices suffered by communities of peoples of color. (One exception noted previously is that the writings of Marcelo de Barros and José Caravias call for a Black theology of the land for Latin America.) Although there has been in Catholic circles an acknowledgment of the oppression of indigenous peoples, Indians and First Nations, and an appreciation of their creation-related spirituality, little has been said of the abuses suffered by Native peoples, African Americans, and Latinos in the United States and Canada, and by *negros* and *indios* in Latin America, that are specifically caused by environmental degradation and devastation. These include diminution of the goods of Earth such as land, water, plants used for food and medicine, and habitat because of the insatiable quest for land, "resources," and affluence in the dominant culture, and the military and industrial measures used to acquire them; and the loss of basic Earth goods such as soil, water, and air to polluting effluents and emissions.

Although some church documents and videos make reference to eco-racist practices, the term itself is not used to highlight the oppression experienced by racial and ethnic minorities and to promote its elimination. Proposals for toxic waste dumps on Indian reservations and toxic waste burning plants in African American neighborhoods; spraying of pesticides harmful to humans on agricultural fields, vineyards, and orchards while they are being worked by Mexican American and Filipino farmworkers; existing and proposed "cancer alley"-type industrial facilities in rural areas populated by minority race poor people—these are some of the existing or proposed eco-racism injustices. The Catholic Church and other religious bodies need to listen to the angry and pleading voices of peoples of color, and respond to them by committing resources and personnel to assist them, by writing statements to the faithful and presenting testimony to governmental bodies to alter their unjust circumstances, and by concrete social actions to eliminate racial oppression. Such church action would help to eradicate the racial, economic, and environmental injustices that are so often ignored or not noticed because the peoples harmed are not sufficient in numbers, financial resources, political power, or church status to pressure for change.

Protestant theologian James Cone writes passionately about the linkage between environmental degradation and the suffering of the African American community. In "Whose Earth Is It, Anyway?"[1] Cone addresses peoples of all colors when he declares:

> People who fight against white racism but fail to connect it to the degradation of the earth are anti-ecological—whether they know it or not. People who struggle against environmental degradation but do not incorporate in it a disciplined and sustained fight against white supremacy are racists—whether they acknowledge it or not. The fight for justice cannot be segregated but must be integrated with the fight for life in all its forms.[2]

In his comments on the importance of environmental problems in the African American community, Cone includes an analogy by theologian Emilie Townes, who describes "'toxic waste landfills in African American communities'" as "'contemporary versions of lynching a whole people.'"[3] The environmental racism data Cone cites includes a United Church of Christ Commission of Racial Justice report in 1987 which found that "forty percent of the nation's commercial hazardous-waste landfill capacity was in three predominantly African American and Hispanic communities."[4]

While individual parishes, some dioceses, and individuals within the church have spoken out against environmental racism and fought against it alongside peoples of color, it has not received sufficient attention from the Catholic Church leadership.

In the United States in particular, ecojustice work requires a special effort to confront and eliminate environmental racism, particularly as exemplified in Earth-related injustices perpetrated against native peoples—American Indians—and African Americans. The former were the original inhabitants of this continent, and lived a spirituality tied to the Earth; they were deprived of their lands, managing only to reserve a part of their original territories in the face of coercion by a dominant and dominating culture. The latter were brought here against their will and forced to work the land for others; they were deprived of the fruits of their labor and of their own nature-based spirituality. Both ethnic groups were and are victims of acts fostering physical and cultural genocide. Both continue to experience the impacts of past injustices related to ownership of the land and use of the Earth's goods. Both are victims of new injustices such as continued deprivation of Earth's goods; poisoning of land, air, and water in areas in which they live and work; and lack of employment in equitable and ecologically sustainable economic activity. Ecojustice means that the environment and the biotic community will be treated fairly; it also means that Earth's benefits will be available to all members of the human family, and that the social structures that determine the extent and division of their distribution will operate fairly.

War and the Environment: War on the Environment

Another important issue in the environmental debate is the impact of war among nations. Because of the devastation it inflicts on the human community in lives and limbs taken from combatants and noncombatants alike and, secondarily, because of its destruction of property and community infrastructure, war deprives humans, the biotic community, and Earth of natural goods needed for the basic survival for all life, and sustainable living and an economic livelihood for human society. War also sets back biotic and cultural communities' evolution and well-being.

The practice of war hardly needs another reason beyond its impacts on humankind and the rest of the biotic community for it to be eliminated as a way of resolving human conflicts. But the threat of long-term environmental impacts might inspire leaders of nations to consider not only the impacts of war that are known already, but also potential additional impacts of actions taken during the conduct of war.

Population, Consumption, and Earth's
Nurturing Capability

At the conclusion of the United Nations' 1992 "Earth Summit" in Rio, a major North–South conflict remained unresolved. The Northern Hemisphere's industrialized and affluent nations accused the South of an irresponsible rate of population growth that threatened Earth's environment because an ever-increasing population had an ever-increasing need for ever-diminishing resources; the Southern Hemisphere's underdeveloped and poorer nations accused the North of a profligate rate of consumption that threatened Earth's environment because it used up far more than its proportional share of Earth's resources, wasted much of what it acquired, and used much more than it needed not only for subsistence but also for a modest standard of living.

An objective observer would agree with both points of view. The Earth's land space is limited not only for human habitation but also for the cultivation of the food and fiber humankind needs; and there are limited Earth goods or "resources" available (Earth is not producing new petroleum, tin, copper, iron, or bauxite, for example; there are fixed quantities of each, and not all are accessible).

The Catholic Church hierarchy has usually ignored population pressures, effectively adapting the southern perspective by admonishing the North (rightly so) to diminish its consumption of Earth's goods, whether in material resources or in energy. From the pew, however, increasing numbers of Catholics, particularly those with backgrounds in the natural and social sciences and theology, are reviewing the data and wondering how humanity can continue on a population-plus-consumption course that will at some point collide colossally with Earth's limited natural capital.

A major stumbling block preventing the institutional church from changing its view on responsible population limitation is its insistence that the primary (and, for some, the only) purpose of sexual intercourse is human reproduction, and this within the context of marriage. Other denominations within Christianity, and other religious faiths, teach a parity of purposes, or a dual purpose, for intercourse, in marriage: an expression of love between husband and wife, and the propagation of offspring. Religious institutions generally teach that intercourse should be reserved for marriage, but where population problems are considered some would also consider birth control measures for unmarried couples, particularly in the light of teenage pregnancies and the AIDS epidemic. The church's advocacy of the right to life of all humans, from womb to tomb, admirably teaches respect for the human person of whatever age, social status, or personal physical circumstance. The church's allowance of birth control practices for Catholics (which need not include acceptance of abortion—voluntarily chosen or involuntarily coerced) would help to limit the human population, and thereby modify one factor (another major one being excessive consumption) that causes environmental devastation and resource depletion.

The issue is obviously very complex, and not an ordinary focus of environmental theology. The population question must be raised, however, because in human societies across the globe admonitions to abstinence and self-restraint are not effective, and a lack of effective birth control practices will lead eventually to a diminution and catastrophic loss of Earth's ability to provide even the necessities of life to humankind and to other members of the biotic community, or to a desperate hope for disease or war to reduce the members of the human family. Neither option is morally acceptable. A "least of available evils" position might have to be assumed by religious leaders who wish for greater human sexual responsibility but simultaneously recognize that it is not happening. In this situation, a prioritizing of principles would be necessary, and the church's life focus would require that it promote practices that would help to sustain the lives of people born into an imperfect world.

Creation Insights: Catholic and Indian Spirituality

In his address to Indians in Phoenix, Arizona, Pope John Paul II recommended to the assembly that they integrate their rich Native American heritage with the Catholic tradition. On numerous other occasions, he affirmed Indian human rights and spiritual insights. The U.S. bishops' 1992 quincentenary pastoral letter also affirmed that Indians of the Americas have had a long history of a spiritual relationship with God, dating to well before the time of contact with the first Christian missionaries.

Several insights of Indian spirituality might stimulate further development of environmental theology in the church in the areas cited. Among these are the sense of kinship with all creatures; a deep respect for Mother Earth; community sharing of regional lands and of individual property in goods; an abiding awareness of the presence of the Spirit; and gratitude to the Spirit for the goods and beauty of creation. Many of these traditional Indian spiritual sensibilities and concrete community practices are part of the Christian heritage as well; the others provide helpful insights into and examples of creation-centered consciousness and creation-concretized responsibility.

Theological Challenges and Considerations

The church—the community of believers—has begun to reflect carefully on scientific findings, environmental concerns, developments in environmental theology, and the relationship of humankind to other species, the Earth, and the Spirit, and to integrate this reflection with theological doctrines developed in past ages. Four hundred years ago, church leaders and theologians were certain that they lived in an Earth-centered universe. In that historical era, the "radical" ideas of Copernicus and Galileo were rejected as contrary to Revelation, the theological tradition, and the *magisterium* of the church; Galileo's ideas were condemned by the Inquisition. Eventually, evidence of a heliocentric system became so overwhelming that church leaders and thinkers had to revise incorrect "facts" about the cosmos and about biblical stories and their interpretation—and reformulate theological perspectives that had been based on previously accepted data.

As evolutionary natural history and human history continue to unfold, other findings and theories in both the natural sciences and the sacred sciences have raised questions about some Christian doctrines or their exposition. An important point to bear in mind here is whether or not these doctrines, in whole or in part, are core doctrines that define the faith. Some might be seen or come to be seen as secondary speculations based on understandings available at particular historical moments and that therefore, like transitional scientific theories, are subject to refinement over time as new data or a better theory becomes available to inquiring human minds. Galileo, although he experienced much personal suffering in his lifetime, eventually was vindicated (although, in the church, only after centuries had passed).

Several important theological issues emerge from the church's engagement with science as a whole and in its environmental particularity. Four of these are presented here as theological considerations that need analysis, prayerful reflection with openness to the guidance of the Creator Spirit, and at least some tentative resolution or projected next steps of reflection. These issues are:

1. The relation of doctrines about a "Fall" and "original sin" with the realization that evolutionary human development from a pre-human stage to an ongoing human stage reveals humans' increasing intellectual and moral capacities

2. The relation of doctrines about a pyramidal hierarchy in nature, with humans at the top and served by all creation below, to the basic biblical teaching that God pronounces everything created "very good," without reference to all of creation having that goodness only for an instrumental

role in service to humans, and scientific understandings of interdependent ecosystems

3. The relation of "redemption" doctrines (linked to the "Fall") to theological understandings that the primary mission and teaching of Jesus were about the "reign of God" that should begin to be realized so that eventually God's will will be done "on Earth as it is in heaven," and

4. The relation of subordinate universe and sacramental universe understandings.

1. The "Fall" and Evolution

It is now well established that death did not come into the world because of human sinfulness; species came into being and became extinct long before humans evolved (consider the dinosaurs as an example). The first humans did not live in a paradise, but in rather harsh natural circumstances wherever they emerged, and had to deal with basic survival issues from the first moment of their evolution. Christian biblical scholars now regard the narratives of Genesis 1–11 as stories rather than histories, as culturally developed myths expressing doctrinal beliefs or moral exhortations rather than historically verifiable accounts of actual events. The Catholic Church accepts theories of evolution as reasonable, with the proviso that the human spirit was a particular creative divine intervention into evolutionary processes occurring on Earth.

Questions for consideration here might be, Are humans more "rising apes" than "fallen angels," that is, are humans developing socially and spiritually through the ages toward fulfillment of a divine vision of what they might reach in the fullness of their humanity, rather than descendants of once-perfect ancestors trying now to replicate a paradisal situation long gone? Is the biblical paradise a vision of what is to come in the future rather than a history of what existed in the past (and a corresponding nostalgia for its return), or is it an attempt to explain why there is evil in the world, a speculation offered by people with no knowledge of evolution or of many other developments in natural and cultural history? Is the fall a historical event or a representative story of human conduct? If the latter, then how might "original sin" be understood? What kind of consciousness did the first humans have? How are humans "co-creators" and engaged in "co-creation" in an evolutionary natural world? Does the concept of co-creators separate humans from nature to some extent, as if they were apart from God's creative action, and creating something apart from the dynamic universe Spirit guides into being? This might seem almost to equate human ingenuity with divine creativity, since natural evolution proceeds ordinarily without human assistance, so human co-creators would be creating not only an added human cultural and social history, but also appropriating and altering past results of God's cosmic creativity, diverting them solely to human use. On the other hand, humans' consciousness, if humans are co-creators, would reflect and participate in divine consciousness and creativity, and people would be the means by which part of the Spirit's vision for the universe comes to pass.

2. Hierarchy and Interdependence in Nature

A significant reason for the devastation of Earth in predominantly Christian nations has been that the planet often has been viewed solely as a place of temporary pilgrimage, a short-term place of preparation for a life to come, the context of the human hope for and working out of "salvation." Additionally, people have been regarded as being above all other creatures. For both reasons, Earth and Earth's creatures were seen as having no value except as they were needed temporarily by humankind.

But people have begun to take seriously the teachings that all creation is "very good" to the Creator, that humans have responsibilities to care for this creation, and that, in fact, humans could not survive without the help of multiple life forms great and small and of a myriad of nonliving entities; all are bound together in interrelationship, interdependence, and ecosystem integrity.

Questions for consideration here might include: Should the human "position" in creation be ideologically shifted from superiority of place to mutuality in roles? Might people accept that they were not placed over creation but are here "to keep and to serve" creation (Gen 2:15)? Would people be able to view other creatures from a horizontal rather than a vertical point of view?

3. "Redemption" and the "Reign of God"

Thomas Berry, Matthew Fox, John Haught, and Ivone Gebara, among others, have urged the Catholic Church to focus more on an "original blessing" or the interdependent and interrelated human role in creation than on redemption/salvation motifs. Their proposal complements the focus on communitarian, rather than individualistic, life in the Bible and in the early Christian community. Most scripture scholars, for their part, see the primary mission of Jesus as the proclamation and initiation of the "reign of God." Jesus speaks of a reign that is here but not entirely fulfilled, that is among us but yet to come, and the only prayer that he gives his followers petitions that God's reign come and that God's will be done "on Earth as it is in heaven." Jesus' followers are charged with the responsibility to work with the Spirit toward the realization of the vision presented in the Lord's Prayer, since God works through human minds and hearts and hands to bring about God's reign, to transform human communities and human history toward their final realization.

The church's social justice teaching is geared toward stimulating the "reign of God" through such practices as a preferential option for the poor; an equitable distribution of Earth's land and Earth's goods; justice among peoples of all races, ethnic groups, nations, and social classes; and care for creation. Pope John Paul II has spoken of humanity's need for an "integral liberation" that includes more than "salvation" in a life to come. Just human communities within a single human family, a goal to be sought on Earth, is a part of that liberation.

In a Christian perspective, in the incarnation God in Jesus reveals and exemplifies the human role in the exhilarating adventure that is the continuing cosmic creation. The human role is part of and complementary to the ongoing unfolding of divine creativity and the universal freedom granted by divine *kenosis;* humans are participants in the cosmic dance of energies, elements, entities, and events, partnered with the Spirit Dancer who leads but also gives freedom and inspiration to those who are open to or guided by the touch of the divine being who is sharing the dance with them. Human activity is "part of" cosmic becoming because humankind is part of natural history, and it is "complementary to" cosmic becoming because humans develop their own social and cultural history. It is both a part of and a complement to cosmic becoming because humans are the self-reflective consciousness of creation who are uniquely endowed to appreciate its complexity and diversity, and therefore can converse in a unique way with the Creator Spirit.

Considerations for further reflection might be a fuller integration of an "integral liberation" with a recognition of human interdependence within the biotic community, and the quest to overcome the apparent conflict between God as Creator and God as Savior when Christians narrowly see the work of Jesus as saving them out of this "world," where the "world" is viewed as the Earth (created by God: Jesus thus "saves" people from out of God's creation, a conflict between divine modes of action) and not as the mindset and practices of any age that contradict the fullness of the reign of God. Rethinking "redemption" does not mean rejecting the tradition or just shifting its foundation from a narrow otherworldly focus to a solely this-world emphasis. It means enriching the tradition by elaborating it and relating it to creation and community consciousness and commitment to a new Earth in a way suggested by Pope John Paul II in his use of the expression "integral liberation": it weaves together the Earth's natural historical dimension and the human community's sociocultural historical dimension with the spiritual dimension, complementing an ultimate redemption of creation in the "kingdom of heaven" with the transitional transformation of creation as the temporal locus of the "reign of God" and presenting an integrated and holistic vision of reality.

4. Subordinate Universe and Sacramental Universe

Awareness of God's immanence in creation and of God's pronouncement of the goodness of creatures have caused people to reflect on what extent, if any, other creatures are to be subordinated to humanity. The fields of quantum physics, biology, and chemistry reveal intricate relationships among the entities that are the objects of their respective studies; psychologists, anthropologists, and sociologists find similar data in human social relationships. Theology and spirituality recognize that God-transcendent is also God-immanent. Understandings of stewardship promote a sense of human responsibility to a creation primarily related to and in service to God, which offers signs of the Creator who brought it into being; the experience of a relational consciousness enables people to regard other members of the biotic community as relatives, or as essential strands of a common web of life.

Confronted by these realities, people might rightly wonder about the appropriateness of regarding the universe as subordinate to human interests: intended for them, designed primarily for them, and in service to them. They might rather see the universe as inherently good in itself, with intricate functions and relationships—conflictive or collaborative—and a sacred site of divine presence, the ultimate temple of the Spirit. In the latter case, the universe is sacramental: revelatory of the Spirit and indicative of the Spirit while having its own integrity and spirit; a sacred place; a blessing; a sign of divine interaction with creation; and the locus and stimulus of experiences of grace.

Questions for consideration would be: To what extent should the teaching of a "sacramental universe" be explored and experienced more fully in the church? How is the "sacramental universe" localized in a "sacramental commons," people's local place of engagement with the Spirit? Are people able to transcend an imbedded anthropocentrism theologically, psychologically, and scientifically in order to develop a relational consciousness and experience the subjectivity of other creatures? What conservation policies and concern for the well-being of human communities and of the biotic community might result with this new consciousness, and how might Earth benefit?

The *Earth Charter:* A Complementary Vision

In 1992, people around the world concerned about environmental degradation and devastation hoped that government leaders gathered in Rio de Janeiro at the United Nations Conference on Environment and Development would develop policies to protect the planet. Maurice Strong, Secretary-General for this "Earth Summit," advocated an *Earth Charter* to complement the United Nations' *Universal Declaration of Human Rights,* but global politics thwarted its development. Strong formed an Earth Council in 1994 to promote sustainable development and in 1995 began to work with Mikhail Gorbachev, President of Green Cross International, to draft the *Earth Charter.* The government of the Netherlands, led by Prime Minister Ruud Lubbers (who later became Director of the World Wide Fund for Nature), provided financial support. In 1995–96 during extensive international consultations, representatives of hundreds of organizations suggested basic principles. In 1997 an international Earth Charter Commission was formed; the latter organized a drafting committee, which presented a Benchmark Draft in the same year. After extensive global consultations and editing, the *Earth Charter* was issued in March 2000 at UNESCO Headquarters in Paris, and in June was officially launched at the Peace Palace in The Hague.[5]

The *Earth Charter* Preamble declares that "in the midst of a magnificent diversity of cultures and life forms we are one human family and one Earth community with a common destiny. We must join together to bring forth a sustainable global society founded on respect for nature, universal human rights, economic justice, and a culture of peace."

The *Earth Charter*'s visionary principles offer a holistic vision of human communities integrated with the biotic community (the community of all life) and respectful of their common Earth home. The document is divided into four parts, each of which has four basic principles; there are sixty-one supporting principles.

The first part, "Respect and Care for the Community of Life," advocates respect for Earth and its diversity of life; the development of democratic societies that are just, participatory, sustainable, and peaceful; and responsibility for future generations. Next, "Ecological Integrity" calls for protection and restoration of Earth's ecosystems; a precautionary approach to environmental impacts; greater study of ecological sustainability; and the adoption of "patterns of production, consumption, and reproduction that safeguard Earth's regenerative capacities, human rights, and community well-being." The third part, "Social and Economic Justice," calls for the eradication of poverty; advocates equitable and sustainable human development; and promotes gender equality and equity "as an ethical, social, and environmental imperative." Finally, "Democracy, Nonviolence and Peace" urges people to "strengthen democratic institutions" and to "promote a culture of tolerance, nonviolence, and peace."

In 2001, when Mikhail Gorbachev was in Italy promoting the *Earth Charter,* Pope John Paul II sent him a message saying he was pleased with "work well done in defense of the environmental heritage"; and in encouraging Gorbachev's goal "to promote greater respect for the resources of the planet which was given by God as a home for a dignified life for all people," the pope sent his blessing.[6]

Earth Charter principles complement religious teachings on environmental responsibility. The *Earth Charter*'s advantage is that it transcends doctrine-limited understandings and can be accepted by people of any faith tradition or by those of a human-ist, rather than a religious, perspective. The advantage of religious teachings advocating "care for creation" or "respect for Mother Earth" is that people within these traditions might become com-mitted to environmental well-being when they see it promoted by their religious leaders as an integral part of their faith.

The *Earth Charter,* then, can be used by Catholics and other Christians to promote care for God's creation. *Earth Charter* principles are compatible with teachings in church statements issued in the past several decades.

Church statements, the writings of scholars, and documents such as the *Earth Charter* all call humankind to a commitment to the evolution and conservation of both natural history and cul-tural history. In natural history, commitment to *evolution* means that people should not intervene in natural processes, occurring in interdependent ecosystems, that are not threatening human well-being; commitment to *conservation* means maintaining existing habitats and species where threats to their existence are, have been, or will be made by past, present, or future human interfer-ence in nonhuman existence and evolution. In human cultural his-tory, commitment to *evolution* means promoting the social and cultural development of distinct, just human communities beyond oppressive ideologies and practices; commitment to *conservation* means retaining those aspects of human development that have promoted human spiritual, social, political, and economic well-being. The two histories are intertwined, which is of particular benefit to humanity.

Environmental theology provides a foundation for people to care for creation, to be compassionate toward those in need, and to be concerned about generations to come. These ideals, expres-sions of faith, should serve to stimulate concrete projects in and for the natural world. Faith-based environmental efforts could have a profound impact on eliminating ecological devastation and enhancing ecological well-being.

7
Care for Creation and Community

The human species is called, as individuals and as a familial community, to care for the Earth and all life. *Care* does not mean to have charge over creation, but to be concerned about its well-being. Consciousness of the needs of creation could prompt people to formulate practical projects to meet them. A Christian tradition permeated by environmental theology could stimulate a transformation of the ways people treat their Earth home and the diversity of life with which they share this home.

Tradition and Transformation

In the span of a few decades, Catholic environmental teachings have undergone a major transformation. The tradition that was dominated by anthropocentrism is developing a foundation for church teachings that integrate human responsibility to care for all creation with human responsibility to be solicitous of the needs of all members of the human family. As this teaching continues to develop, it will impact the church, the broader Christian community, and the public at large. People will assess more objectively their patterns of pollution and consumption, and their responsibilities to humanity, to Earth and all Earth's creatures, and to God. Such an assessment, when accompanied by an enhanced spiritual sense of the presence of God-immanent, and when incorporated into con-

130 What Are They Saying About Environmental Theology?

crete historical projects of social and ecological transformation, will lead to a renewed Earth and to renewed communities on Earth.

In issues of science, ecology, and theology, people must engage in an "open search for truth," as Pope John Paul II has stated, while "distinguishing the valid elements in the tradition from false and erroneous ones, or from obsolete forms which can be usefully replaced by others more suited to the times" (*Centesimus Annus* §50).

A tradition in transformation becomes in turn a transforming tradition. It begins to have more concrete impact on the world in which it is evolving. In the case of environmental theology, people begin to formulate principles to guide concrete contextual projects in their human communities and in the bioregions in which these communities are situated.

Contextual Commitments to Creation

Faith-based environmental organizations around the world and parishes with environmental consciousness have been engaged in a variety of practical projects to enhance their regional commons and their local community. Their works provide models for similar groups in equivalent settings. Two clusters of groups merit recognition: in the global commons, the recipients of the "Sacred Gifts for a Living Planet" award from the Alliance of Religions and Conservation (ARC), an affiliate of the World Wide Fund for Nature (WWF); and the diverse parishes honored by the U.S. Conference of Catholic Bishops Environmental Justice Program: "Parish Models of Environmental Justice"; "Small Grant Program" award recipients; and "Regional Grant Awards" recipients.[1]

ARC/WWF

In 2000, the first "Sacred Gifts for a Living Planet" awards were presented in Bhaktapur, Nepal, by Prince Philip, the Duke of Edinburgh (and husband of Queen Elizabeth II), to honor twenty-six faith-based environmental efforts that emerged from eleven different religious traditions. The U.S. projects honored include:

1. "Columbia River Pastoral Letter Project" from the Northwestern United States/Southwestern Canada, which was developing the bishops' bioregional pastoral letter (described in chapter 3).

2. "United Methodist Campaign for a Dioxin-Free Environment" spearheaded by the Women's Division of the church. This effort seeks to eliminate the use of all chlorine paper products in Methodist churches, to promote the use of chlorine-free paper across the United States by churches, communities, businesses, and individual citizens, and to pressure the paper industry toward environmentally responsible manufacturing processes. Church members were concerned about carcinogenic dioxins released into the environment by the manufacture and burning of chlorine paper.

3. "Glinodo Earth Force Program" of the Benedictine Sisters of Erie, Pennsylvania. This environmental education program is based in thirty schools. Lake Erie is part of the Great Lakes system, which has one-fifth of the world's fresh water. The program has students monitor water quality and engage in civic action to change public policy and pollution practices and to promote sustainable freshwater management.

4. "Episcopal Power and Light Ministry," an Episcopal Church program based in California, seeks to diminish global warming and improve energy efficiency and economic benefits in churches across the United States. EP&L, which encourages the installation of alternative energy sources in church institutions, organized a demonstration project in which the year 2000 U.S. General

Convention of the Episcopal Church, with 15,000 participants, was powered by renewable energy.

5. "Environmental Audit for Conservative and Reform Judaism," organized by leaders of the United Synagogue of Conservative Judaism and the Union of American Hebrew Congregations (Reform), is developing the most significant Jewish environmental project in U.S. history. These two branches of Judaism, which include 80 percent of Jews in the country, are asking all synagogues and related educational and charitable organizations to have an environmental audit, cut energy consumption, and thereby reduce CO_2 emissions to Kyoto Protocol levels. Members of these congregations will strive to reduce energy consumption in their homes and businesses and to use wood products harvested sustainably; Home Depot, owned by a member of one of the congregations, has become a main U.S. supplier of certified wood products.

USCC

The projects recognized by the U.S. bishops' Environmental Justice Program care for creation in diverse ways:

1. The "BioBox Project" in inner-city Denver Catholic schools has sixth-grade students put together boxes with artifacts and information about their bioregion, and exchange them with students from other regions. Students learn about their region's unique characteristics and develop a sense of creation's sacredness.

2. In the "Cycle of Life Project" in St. Mary's School in the Knoxville, Tennessee, diocese, students use organic gardening done in compost piles to beautify their school landscape and provide vegetables for local food programs for the poor.

3. The "De La Roca Saldrá Agua" community garden project in Bridgeport, Connecticut, transformed a trash-filled abandoned city lot into a neighborhood garden, particularly for use by the elderly of the community.

4. The Philadelphia Archdiocese participates in the Interfaith Coalition on Energy, which uses workbooks to help parish members conduct an energy audit and establish efficient energy use.

5. The "Mothers of East L.A.," which includes members from Resurrection Parish, Los Angeles, prevented construction of a hazardous waste incinerator and a toxic chemical cleaning plant near their community.

6. In Santa Fe, New Mexico, the St. Charles Borromeo School developed "Solar Energy—God's Engine for Creation" to educate elementary and middle school students about the use of alternative energy to promote environmental responsibility.

7. The "Save Our Water" program of the Diocese of Rockville Centre, New York, promotes chemical-free care of residential lawns to maintain aquifer water quality.

These representative projects from across the United States provide concrete examples of the types of programs and practices that might be undertaken by other parishes, schools, and communities to care for God's creation and promote their own financial and ecological well-being. Individuals, parish communities or committees, seminaries, educational institutions, and local businesses—or any combination thereof—should consider the possibility of replicating the efforts just cited, or developing their own innovative projects through a careful analysis of local natural and community characteristics and of perceived problems and needs.

Communities of Faith: Commitments to Creation

People as integrated communities are called to be concerned about and compassionate toward those in greatest need in the human community. They should have a preferential option for the economically poor and for the ethnically, racially, and otherwise socially oppressed. A just distribution and redistribution of human property in land and goods would both express this option and enhance familial bonds.

Humankind is able, more than other creatures, to integrate knowledge of physical laws with knowledge of distinct species with diverse ecosystem needs. Through telescopes, microscopes, and computer modeling, people can see into the heights and the depths and learn ever more about the vastness and intricacies of the cosmos. With expanding knowledge and enhanced understanding, humanity can stand increasingly more in awe of the phenomena of creation, in humility before the Creator who brings it into being, and in wonderment that they have been entrusted with responsible freedom to care for it.

With this in mind, Christians aware of the presence of God in the universe and in the commons, who realize that their responsibility within and for creation as images of a loving Creator is "an essential part of their faith," will seek to be caretakers of creation. A parish or congregation, as a whole or through its individual parishioners, can minister to its own members, to the broader social community, and to the integrated Earth community. Some suggestions follow for this ministry.

Twelve Projects for Creation Care

1. Develop Environmental Inventories. Faith communities should undertake structural and landscape inventories to determine if their buildings are energy efficient, if their insulation can be improved, if their heating and cooling systems need repair or replacement, if more trees (which beautify places and cleanse the air) should be planted to provide summer shade and winter shield, and if lawns can be sown with native grasses, which require little or no maintenance (thereby saving water, eliminating lawn chemicals, and reducing gasoline for lawn mowers: all of which save energy resources, money, the environment, and health).

2. *Use Appropriate Construction Materials and Alternative Energy.* New buildings should utilize appropriate alternative building materials, and incorporate long-term energy conservation measures such as energy efficient windows and passive and active solar energy techniques and technologies. Older structures should be evaluated to see the extent to which retrofitting measures might make them similarly more energy conserving. Churches should assess their energy needs regionally, and jointly seek alternative solar and wind energy sources—ideally in conjunction with agriculturalists and local communities: unutilized regional farm spaces can provide locations for windmills and banks of solar collectors; workers in local rural communities could be employed manufacturing them. Electric cooperatives could be founded to operate regional utilities in the interests of regional communities rather than primarily for the profit of speculators who own or manage distant utility corporations.

3. *Diminish or Eliminate Use of Minerals and Materials Threatening Life or Health.* Faith communities should diminish the use of gold and other materials whose extraction or refinement harms the Earth and the health of people and other creatures. Just as asbestos once was *installed* in elementary schools to protect children, but now is being *removed* to protect children, so, too, since chemicals such as cyanide used in gold mining harm the biotic community, and since most gold is used for jewelry, gold should be reused or alternatives to it should be found so that creation, agricultural operations, wildlife, and Native sacred sites might be conserved, and a more healthful environment be restored.

4. Restore and Conserve Bioregions. Members of local communities should explore ways to work with scientists, government officials, environmentalists, and business owners to restore and conserve their bioregion. Local knowledge of an ecosystem has been developed and passed on over generations in families and in the workplace by means of oral and written traditions. It can be linked with specific scientific data and government policies so that communities might adapt to and work well with the ecosystem upon which they rely, to which they are related, and for which they have a responsibility.

5. Develop Restoration Projects Good for Jobs, Species, and the Environment. Environmental restoration projects for salmon, trout, redwoods, saguaro cactus, and other threatened or endangered animal or plant species can provide jobs while conserving environmental integrity for the well-being of humans and other creatures of God. Environmental pollution from mining and oil spills, and environmental degradation from clearcut logging practices and open pit mining operations can be ameliorated, and good, long-term, and well-paying jobs can be created, by requiring a best-case cleanup of afflicted areas.

6. Recycle for the Environment and for Community Programs. Recycling campaigns (newspapers, aluminum cans, corrugated cardboard, glass) should be undertaken to raise needed funds for youth groups and other programs while promoting conservation. Faith communities and educational institutions should use chlorine-free recycled paper to eliminate the dumping of toxic paper plant effluents into rivers.

7. Actively Promote Justice for the Poor and for Ethnic and Racial Minorities. People have a particular responsibility for their species, which is their extended family, to ensure that all its members receive an equitable share of Earth's goods. The "least of Jesus' brethren," those deprived of food, drink, clothing, shelter, adequate medical care, and judicial fairness (see Matt 25:31–46) because of their poverty or minority status in the dominant culture should have not only their basic needs but a fair share of reasonable wants satisfied. Christian parishes should seek to overcome economic and color barriers to ensure that this occurs. White supremacy against other races, and the current economic class war against the poor, are attitudes and actions that are not always overt: prejudice can take covert forms that, although not as dramatic and visible to the public eye, have similar or worse impacts on the psyche and the physical, social, and economic well-being of the poor and of peoples of color.

8. Analyze and Alter Unjust Economic Structures. In the United States, the wealthiest and most powerful nation in the world, there should be no hunger or homelessness or lack of basic health care. Yet, millions of people in the United States experience one or all of these forms of basic deprivation. "Minimum" wages guarantee poverty; minimal or no health benefits exacerbate it. Economic democracy is at least as important as political democracy. Earth's goods should provide for the needs of all, but this provision is impeded or stymied by an existing economic structure controlled by and primarily benefiting a few people instead of the vast majority. A living wage and safe working conditions, adequate housing, and universal health care are missing from this structure, and should become part of it. Workers and those wanting to be workers should explore founding cooperatives and joining responsible labor unions in order to work for economic justice. The oft-used phrase in Catholic social teaching, which has particular importance in ensuring that Earth's goods are distributed equitably (while not harming Earth in their acquisition, their alteration in production processes, and their disposition) is that there is a "universal destination of goods" (that is, one might add, a "universal" destination for humans of those goods which are appropriately designated for the human family; the goods as a whole are also intended to meet the needs of other creatures). These ideals should be much more forcefully advocated and modeled in Catholic institutions such as hospitals, church offices, and educational institutions. Catholic seminaries and universities should teach them; parishes and community organizations should help to make them realities.

9. Reduce and Eliminate Harmful Chemical Inputs. Corporate and family agricultural operations, and church, government, commercial, and industrial properties often use fertilizers, herbicides, and insecticides to enhance landscapes or increase the production of food and fiber. These additives to the natural environment are harmful to people (those who apply them, especially farmers, farm workers, and hobby farmers; those who unknowingly consume them), pets, water supplies, and beneficial soil organisms. Their use should be greatly reduced; weed and insect infestations often can be diminished or eradicated by the use of natural biological controls, alternative species, or varieties of seed, and alternative methods of cultivation that benefit the soil and decrease wind and soil erosion. Faith communities and individuals should support local and regional organic farmers at farmers' markets, and encourage managers of local supermarkets to buy locally. As much as possible, church-related schools should buy locally grown organic produce, and officials of public schools should be encouraged to do so also. The diets of children in all schools should be made healthier by eliminating excessive fried foods and sugar, and replacing soft drink dispensers with water and juice vending machines. Parents should provide healthy diets at home and press for them in educational institutions.

10. Evaluate the Link between Population, Consumption, and Environmental Issues. There is a growing concern among analysts of environmental degradation that the primary cause is not simply population *or* consumption. In some way, each contributes to depletion of available goods to meet human needs and of available land on which to grow them or from which to gather them, and promotes diminished possibilities of providing for human (and other creatures') needs into the future. Geographic and cultural factors impact both: population might be more of an issue in some parts of the world, consumption in others. Earth as home cannot have any living space—habitat—added on to it out into space, as a family might add on to its dwelling; neither might Earth as a source of needed minerals have those restocked, as the manager of a clothing store might do in a place of business to meet customers' needs. Advocates of unrestricted population growth and advocates of unlimited consumption and unlimited "economic growth" and their adversaries in each arena must come to terms with the impacts made, on Earth and on human well-being and on the ability of both to survive, by increased energy consumption, mineral extraction, accelerated petroleum depletion, forest loss, and diminished water supplies. Responsible family planning and responsible use of the goods of the Earth are not exclusive, but inclusive options. As such complementarity is contemplated, church leaders and theologians must be open to the signs of the times and the inspiration of the Spirit to explore ways in which ecological needs and spiritual relationships are intertwined. On this issue, the church might well be at a watershed moment, much as it was when scientists using mathematics and telescopes observed that the sun, not Earth, was at the center of the planetary system. As the reflective consciousness of the universe, people as individuals and as the community of faith—the church—must come to terms with this extremely pressing population-consumption combination of human actions. Church leaders need not relinquish their teachings about abortion, but they must place their moral concern about the "right to life" within a context in which Earth might not be able to provide for the life of children being born today if population growth continues at current rates; neither would they have to alter their teaching about reserving sexual intercourse for marriage, but they must more forcefully promote not only sexual responsibility but population responsibility among couples. The current impasse results in people in the Northern Hemisphere blithely continuing to consume more than their just share of Earth's goods and benefits while blaming the South for environmental problems; and in people in the Southern Hemisphere (at times fearful, because of poverty and infant mortality resulting from poverty, poor health care, polluted water, and minimal water treatment) having more children than their nation can provide for while condemning the North for taking and consuming southern goods and destroying southern ecologies.

11.   Explore and Implement the Just Distribution and Redistribution of Property in Land. The Catholic bishops on occasion have called for a graduated or progressive land tax (in *Strangers and Guests* and in *Economic Justice for All,* among other places). This type of tax was part of U.S. policy early in the history of the republic (having been advocated by Thomas Jefferson and Thomas Paine) and would be a contemporary way of implementing the biblical Jubilee practice that the land should be periodically redistributed. Such a *re*distribution of land as property complements a just distribution of property in future economic arrangements. If property is only distributed equitably from this moment onward, those who have currently a gross advantage in property and goods (and their descendants) will retain that economic (and thus political) advantage in ages to come. A progressive land tax (enabling retention of an amount of land needed by a family operation to provide a good standard of living for owner-operated/owner-occupied farms, for example), complemented by a progressive estate tax and a progressive income tax (and by such policies as a graduated grazing fee for private ranchers' livestock using public lands), would help to provide for the needs of all and promote political and economic democracy.

12.   Form Integrated and Active Alliances and Associations. Faith groups should reach out to environmental groups for mutual education and joint projects. Environmental organizations would provide expertise about environmental issues and community projects to care for the environment. Church members would offer their consciousness of the commons as God's creation, and their awareness of local employment needs. Both would be committed to restoring and conserving ecologically important areas while promoting economically sustainable communities.

The Bible teaches that humans are images of God. They are that part of creation that can best reveal God's creativity, God's loving solicitude, and God's integrating consciousness to the world. People are called to recognize God's presence and to be the sign and reflection of God's presence in creation. People also witness for the world who God is, as far, that is, as they can discern that, and in the extent to which they so act within their human limitations. Just as they live in a sacramental universe, humans are called to be sacramental beings in that universe; their lives, words, and actions should help to make God known in concrete ways in human and natural history. When people walk with God, conscious that God is present to and with them, with God's grace they can present God in new ways in the world.

People are called to participate lovingly and responsibly in the ongoing process of creation. They are called to fulfill this responsibility with grateful love and concern for all the created cosmos. They should remember that what God has created is good, and work with God to integrate that goodness. People must have a loving solicitude for all around them, and while meeting human needs strive to respect *all* of creation, not only those parts of it that are needed for human survival and well-being, sometimes provided through the gift of their lives. Within the human family, people's relational social presence (their interaction with others as a community) enables them to be signs to each other of God's presence.

People are a part of Nature, and use natural goods to meet their needs. In doing so, they have a great responsibility to God, to the present and future human community, to the broader biotic community, and to Earth as a whole in the ways they gather and use natural goods. People must care for all creation, even while recognizing its dynamic being and the conflicts and collaborations that are part of the evolution of life.

People are immersed in the natural world, not transcendent to it or enthroned over it. At times, they have to change Earth's terrain to meet their needs; they should not change it solely to satisfy insatiable wants. People should preserve and conserve Earth and respect its community of life, and restore, where possible, areas where they have adapted Earth to themselves by altering its habitat and adversely affecting Earth's species to meet human needs and wants. Appropriately designed and integrated human alterations to the landscape, by contrast, can work with the existing and evolving ecosystem. Communities and farms, commercial enterprises and industrial operations can be conceptualized, contextualized, constructed, and concretized in places and ways that efficiently use regional "resources" without harming regional ecologies. As a species and as images of God, people can become native to their place, whether or not they were born in the area in which they now live and work, if they become attuned to its natural rhythms and conscious of its spiritual realities.

People are called, then, to be the caring consciousness of creation—and citizens of compassionate cultural communities. Natural history and cultural history, concern for Earth and concern for humankind in whole and in part, must be woven together. People must transcend the anthropocentric attitudes and practices so characteristic of much of the faith community, the scientific community, and the business and political communities, and they must replace avarice and competition with generosity and collaboration. This would be in humanity's long-term self-interest, because without bioregional ecological balance, and global ecological and economic balance, Earth will not survive. More importantly, when people recognize their interdependence with each other and all creation, and are integrated and interrelated as a human family and as children of the Spirit and of the nurturing Earth, they will truly fulfill the deepest meaning of "images of God." Then they will walk with the Spirit and work with the Spirit toward a new heaven and a new Earth, in which there truly would be peace with the Spirit Creator and peace with all creation.

Notes

Introduction: Crisis and Concern

1. *Earth* here and throughout the text is capitalized as one of the planets of the solar system; to distinguish it from the soil; to highlight it as humanity's particular home; to foster its care; and to indicate its importance in God's creation as the cosmic locus of the incarnation. The Appalachian bishops use this convention in *At Home in the Web of Life* (Webster Springs, WV: Catholic Committee of Appalachia, 1995).

2. The life and work of Francis and Benedict are well known; less familiar is the quote from Augustine approvingly quoted by Aquinas: "In the words of Augustine: '...some people presume to find fault with many things in this world, through not seeing the reasons for their existence. For though not required for the furnishing of our house, these things are necessary for the perfection of the universe.'"(*Summa Theologica,* I, Q. 72, Art. 1; quoted in *Basic Writings of Saint Thomas Aquinas,* edited and annotated with an introduction by Anton C. Pegis [New York: Random House, 1945], p. 667; see St. Augustine, *De Genesi Contra Manich.,* I, 16 [PL 34: 185].)

3. Léon-Joseph Cardinal Suenens, *Memories and Hopes,* trans. Elena French (Dublin, Ireland: Veritas Publications, 1992), p. 155.

4. Ibid., p. 351.

1. Creation, Creatures, and Community Consideration

1. Quotations from Vatican II documents are taken from Walter M. Abbott, S.J., ed., *The Documents of Vatican II* (New York: Herder and Herder, 1966).

143

2. Léon-Joseph Cardinal Suenens, *Memories and Hopes,* trans. Elena French (Dublin, Ireland: Veritas Publications, 1992), p. 155.

3. Ibid., p. 151.

4. "Rights of the Rural Poor," *Origins,* Vol. 8: No. 34, p. XXX.

5. "The Pope's Homily in Rural America," *Origins,* Vol. 9: No. 18, p. XXX.

6. Pope John Paul II, *The Ecological Crisis: A Common Responsibility* (Washington, DC: United States Catholic Conference, 1990). The message was first released on December 8, 1989, but became the pope's "World Day of Peace Message" on January 1, 1980. The heading at the beginning of the document is "Peace with God the Creator, Peace with All Creation."

7. Pope John Paul II, "Respect for Human Rights: The Secret of True Peace," *Origins,* Vol. 28: No. 28, pp. 489–93.

8. "Address of Pope John Paul II to the Native Americans in Phoenix, Arizona," *Origins,* Vol. 17: No. 17, pp. 295–98.

9. "Homily of the Holy Father Pope John Paul II," Vatican Web site: http://www.vatican.va/holy_father/john_paul_ii/homilies/2002/documents/hf_jp-ii_hom_20020730_canonization-guatemala_en.html.

10. "Homily of the Holy Father Pope John Paul II," Vatican Web site: http://www.vatican.va/holy_father/john_paul_ii/homilies/2002/documents/hf_jp-ii_hom_20020731_canonization-mexico_en.html.

11. Press copy of the address, distributed at UNCED, June 4, 1992. This writer participated in UNCED as a journalist, and in the World Conference of Indigenous Peoples held in Rio just prior to this Earth Summit.

12. Renato Martino, UNCED address.

13. William Bole, "Renewed Calls for an 'Ecological Conversion,'" *Our Sunday Visitor,* Vol. 91: No. 21, September 22, 2002, p. 5.

14. United States Catholic Conference, *Catechism of the Catholic Church* (Washington, DC: United States Catholic Conference, 1994).

15. Ibid., part 3, sec. 2, chap. 2, art. 7.

2. Common Ground and Common Good

1. The Dominican Episcopal Conference, *Pastoral Letter on the Relationship of Human Beings to Nature*. Published in Drew Chris-

tiansen, S.J., and Walter Grazer, eds., *"And God Saw That It Was Good": Catholic Theology and the Environment* (Washington, DC: United States Catholic Conference, 1996), pp. 259–74.

2. Guatemalan Bishops' Conference, *The Cry for Land.* Published in Christiansen and Grazer, *"And God Saw That It Was Good,"* pp. 275–93.

3. U.S. Catholic Bishops, *Renewing the Earth: An Invitation to Reflection and Action in Light of Catholic Social Teaching* (Washington, DC: United States Catholic Conference, November 14, 1991). In the national U.S. bishops' letter, and in most regional letters from the United States and Canada, paragraphs are not numbered. Section citations will be used, as available, for reference in these cases.

4. I. Signs of the Times, opening paragraph, p. 1.

5. Ibid., p. 1.

6. I., A. Aims of This Statement, p. 2.

7. I., B. Justice and the Environment, p. 2.

8. I., D. A Call to Reflection and Action, p. 3.

9. Ibid.

10. II. The Biblical Vision of God's Good Earth, A. The Witness of the Hebrew Scriptures, p. 4.

11. II., B. The Gospel Message, p. 5.

12. III. Catholic Social Teaching and Environmental Ethics, A. A Sacramental Universe, p. 6.

13. Ibid.

14. Ibid.

15. III., B. Respect for Life, p. 7.

16. III., D. A New Solidarity, p. 7.

17. III. E. Universal Purpose of Created Things, p. 8.

18. IV. Theological and Pastoral Concerns, C. Christian Love, p. 11.

19. III., H. Consumption and Population, p. 9; the bishops reference statements by Pope Paul VI and Pope John Paul II relative to population increases being an impediment to development.

20. V. God's Stewards and Co-Creators, B. New Actions, p. 13.

21. V. God's Stewards and Co-Creators, D. A Word of Hope, p. 14.

22. U.S. Catholic Bishops, *Sharing Catholic Social Teaching: Challenges and Directions.* In *Origins,* Vol. 28: No. 7, pp. 102–6.

23. Ibid, p. 104.

24. U.S. Catholic Bishops, *1992: A Time for Reconciling and Recommitting Ourselves as a People—Pastoral Reflections on the V Centenary and Native American People* (November 1991).

25. U.S. Catholic Bishops, *Statement of U.S. Catholic Bishops on American Indians* (May 4, 1977) (Washington, DC: United States Catholic Conference, 1977).

26. Native peoples of the Americas prefer the designation "Indian" when they are referred to in a general way as the first inhabitants of the Americas, and prefer over that term the specific name of their own nation/people (e.g., Lakota, Hopi, Cree, etc.) when a particular reference is made to them as individuals or as a community.

27. I. A Time for Remembering.

28. II. A Time for Reconciliation, A. Inculturation.

29. III. A Time for Recommitment, A. Public Advocacy.

30. III., B. Respecting Treaty Rights.

31. U.S. Catholic Bishops, *Global Climate Change: A Plea for Dialogue, Prudence and the Common Good* (Washington, DC: United States Catholic Conference, 2001), p. 1.

32. Ibid, p. 8.

33. Ibid, p. 17.

34. Ibid, p. 1.

35. Ibid, p. 11.

36. Ibid, p. 12.

37. Ibid, p. 7.

38. Ibid, p. 10.

39. Ibid, p. 15.

40. Ibid, p. 7.

41. Ibid, p. 6.

3. Sacramental and Communal Creation

1. Appalachian Catholic Bishops, *This Land Is Home to Me—A Pastoral Letter on Powerlessness in Appalachia by the Catholic Bishops of the Region,* 4th ed. (Webster Springs, WV: Catholic Committee of Appalachia, 1990).

2. I: The Land and Its People, p. 3.

3. I, "Coal," p. 5.

4. Ibid., p. 6.

5. I, "The Worship of an Idol," p. 7.

6. I, "Appalachia as a Symbol," p. 10.

7. Ibid.

8. II, The Answer of Jesus and His Church, p. 15.

9. Ibid.

10. III: Facing the Future: A Process of Dialogue and Testing, p. 22.

11. Conclusion, p. 25.

12. Midwestern Catholic Bishops, *Strangers and Guests: Toward Community in the Heartland, a Regional Catholic Bishops' Statement on Land Issues,* May 1, 1980 (Sioux Falls, SD: Heartland Project, 1980). This writer served as the editor and principal writer of the pastoral letter authored by the bishops; the other writers were Stephana Landwehr, David Ostendorf, and Marty Strange, who wrote the first draft and contributed to the second. Comments on the first draft that were recorded during scores of meetings throughout the region, and amendments from the bishops, were incorporated into the second and succeeding drafts, and the bishops, as authors, finalized and issued the pastoral letter.

13. Official text of the papal homily distributed to the press at Living History Farms, Des Moines, Iowa, October 4, 1979. At the request of Bishop Maurice Dingman of Des Moines, this writer served as the drafter of the homily sent to Pope John Paul II in advance of his trip to the United States. *Origins,* Vol. 9: No. 18, pp. 293–94.

14. Northwestern Christian Leaders, "A Public Declaration: To the Tribal Councils and Traditional Spiritual Leaders of the Indian and Eskimo Peoples of the Pacific Northwest." Flyer (one page) distributed throughout the region's churches and through Indian and Eskimo organizations.

15. Appalachian Catholic Bishops, *At Home in the Web of Life* (Webster Springs, WV: Catholic Committee of Appalachia, 1995).

16. Sustainable Communities, p. 3.

17. A Culture of Death or Life? p. 5.

18. I. The Land and Its People, Creation Is God's Word, Revelation of the Forests, p. 15.

19. Natural and Social Ecology, p. 7.

20. I., p. 12.

21. Ibid.

22. II. The Bible and the Church's Teaching, Love for Creation, p. 28.

23. II., Ownership, p. 35.

24. III. The Call of the Spirit, Sustainable Ownership, p. 47.

25. Ibid.

26. III., In Conclusion, p. 57.

27. New Mexico Catholic Bishops, *Reclaiming the Vocation to Care for the Earth,* May 11, 1998. *Origins,* Vol. 28: No. 4, pp. 63–64.

28. The preceding statements are from *Reclaiming the Vocation to Care for the Earth,* p. 63.

29. The quotations in this paragraph are from *Reclaiming the Vocation to Care for the Earth,* p. 64.

30. Alberta Catholic Bishops, *Celebrate Life: Care for Creation—The Alberta Bishops' Letter on Ecology for October 4, 1998* (Edmonton, Alberta: Western Catholic Reporter Web site: http://www.wcr.ab.ca/bin/eco-lett.htm, 1998).

31. Ibid., Biblical Ecological Vision.

32. Ibid.

33. Ibid.

34. Learning from Catholic Social Teaching.

35. Ibid.

36. Ibid.

37. Ibid.

38. Ibid.

39. Urgent Need for Action: An Alberta Reflection.

40. Ibid.

41. A New Beginning.

42. Ibid.

43. Ibid.

44. Boston Province Catholic Bishops, *And God Saw That It Was Good—A Pastoral Letter of the Bishops of the Boston Province* (Boston, MA: Archdiocese of Boston, October 4, 2000); *Origins,* Vol. 30: No. 20, pp. 318–20.

45. III. New England Concerns.

46. Ibid.

47. Ibid.

48. II. Church Teaching.

49. IV. An Environmental Examination of Conscience: Invitation and Challenge.

50. Ibid.

51. Ibid.

52. Columbia River Watershed Catholic Bishops, *The Columbia River Watershed: Caring for Creation and the Common Good—An International Pastoral Letter by the Bishops of the Region* (Seattle, WA: Columbia River Pastoral Letter Project, January 8, 2001). The letter was printed in its entirety in the March 8, 2001, issue of the U.S. bishops' publication *Origins,* Vol. 30: No. 38, pp. 609–19. This writer served as the project writer for this pastoral letter authored by the bishops. More than one hundred people offered suggestions and phrasing for the letter: as invited consultants for the first draft; as Steering Committee members; during the "Readings of the Signs of the Times" meetings and "Listening Sessions" held throughout the region; and as respondents to the draft on the project Web site: www.columbiariver.org. The bishops, as authors, amended and issued the pastoral letter.

53. I. The Rivers of Our Moment; Spiritual and Social Consciousness, p. 5.

54. Ibid.

55. II. The Rivers through Our Memory; Church Teachings about the Land, p. 9.

56. II.; Religious Traditions, p. 7.

57. II.; The Columbia and the Common Good, p. 8.

58. Introductory section; Caring for Our Common Home, p. 2.

59. II.; Living Water, p. 8.

60. Ibid., p. 9.

61. II.; Church Teachings about the Land, p. 9.

62. III. The Rivers of Our Vision; Spiritual Vision, p. 11.

63. III. Convictions That Underscore the Need to Care for the Earth, p. 12.

64. IV. The Rivers as Our Responsibility, p. 13.

65. *And God Saw That It Was Good,* I. Biblical Basis.

66. Alaska Catholic Bishops, *A Catholic Perspective on Subsistence: Our Responsibility toward Alaska's Bounty and Our Human Family,* April 12, 2002: http://www.archdioceseofanchorage.org/a catholic perspective on subsis.htm. Published in *Origins* with the erroneous title *Alaska's Bounty and the Human Family: A Catholic Perspective on*

Subsistence, although in the introductory paragraph to the letter the correct title is used. *Origins,* Vol. 31: No. 45, pp. 745–52.

67. Ibid., p. 746.

68. Ibid., p. 747.

69. All citations in this paragraph are from *A Catholic Perspective on Subsistence,* p. 747.

70. Ibid.

71. All quotations from this paragraph are from *A Catholic Perspective on Subsistence,* p. 748.

72. Ibid.

73. Ibid., pp. 748–49.

74. Ibid., p. 749.

75. Ibid.

76. Ibid.

77. Ibid., pp. 749–50.

4. Transforming Tradition and Conserving Creation: Northern Visions

1. Native peoples with roots in what is now the Americas are technically neither "Indian" nor "American." Traditional bearers of their traditions still use the term "Indian" when referring to themselves or their people, not "Native American" or "First Nations," except as necessary to communicate with government entities or, sometimes, with the public in general. While acknowledging that they are neither "American" nor "Indian," the first Native delegates to the United Nations International Human Rights Commission, in Geneva, Switzerland, who were traveling as the International Indian Treaty Council, decided that "Indian" was the name by which they were oppressed, and "Indian" would be the name under which they would become free.

2. Thomas Mails, *Fools Crow: The Fascinating Memoir of the Great Ceremonial Chief of the Teton Sioux* (New York: Avon Books, 1980), p. 45.

3. John Neihardt, then the Poet Laureate of Nebraska, was writing a series of epic poems about the settling of the West. He wanted to have a poem celebrating Native peoples. He heard about Black Elk, sought him out, and interviewed him over the course of some two years. *Black Elk Speaks,* which Neihardt edited, was the result.

4. Raymond J. DeMallie, *The Sixth Grandfather: Black Elk's Teachings Given to John G. Neihardt* (Lincoln: University of Nebraska Press, 1985), p. 266.

5. Joseph Epes Brown, *The Sacred Pipe: Black Elk's Account of the Seven Rites of the Oglala Sioux* (New York: Penguin Books, 1976), p. 46.

6. Ibid., p. 64.

7. Ibid., p. 75.

8. Ibid., p. 97.

9. Ibid., p. 115.

10. Mails, *Fools Crow,* p. 53.

11. Ibid., p. 45.

12. Ibid., p. 136.

13. Ibid., p. 3.

14. Ibid., p. 202.

15. Ibid., p. 190.

16. Ibid., p. 81.

17. Ibid., p. 75.

18. Ibid., p. 109.

19. My own work in this area is based on my association with traditional Native spiritual leaders and human rights activists through my involvement with the International Indian Treaty Council, a Non-Governmental Organization (NGO) accredited to the United Nations. I discussed the complementarity of these religious worldviews in *The Spirit of the Earth: A Theology of the Land* (Mahwah, NJ: Paulist Press, 1984).

20. Matthew Fox, *Original Blessing: A Primer in Creation Spirituality* (Santa Fe, NM: Bear & Co., 1986), p. 11.

21. Ibid., pp. 18–19.

22. Ibid., pp. 19, 46.

23. Ibid., p. 26.

24. Ibid., p. 48.

25. Ibid., p. 300.

26. Ibid., p. 111.

27. Ibid., pp. 38–39.

28. Ibid., p. 69.

29. Ibid., p. 90.

30. Matthew Fox, *Creation Spirituality: Liberating Gifts for the Peoples of the Earth* (San Francisco, CA: HarperSanFrancisco, 1991), p. 31.

31. Ibid., p. 35.

32. Ibid., p. 41.

33. Ibid., p. 52.

34. Ibid., p. 70.

35. Ibid., p. 111.

36. Ibid., p. 140.

37. Rosemary Radford Ruether, *Gaia and God: An Ecofeminist Theology of Earth Healing* (San Francisco, CA: HarperSanFrancisco, 1994), pp. 2–3.

38. Ibid., p. 3.

39. Ibid.

40. Ibid., p. 4.

41. Ibid., p. 206.

42. Ibid., p. 12.

43. Ibid., p. 86.

44. Ibid., p. 21.

45. Ibid., p. 222.

46. Ibid., p. 227.

47. Ibid., p. 48.

48. Ibid., p. 101.

49. Ibid.

50. Ibid.

51. Ibid., p. 188.

52. Ibid., pp. 207–8.

53. Ibid., p. 233.

54. Ibid., p. 258.

55. Ibid., p. 256.

56. Ibid., p. 263.

57. Ibid., p. 264–65.

58. Rosemary Radford Ruether, ed., *Women Healing Earth: Third World Women on Ecology, Feminism, and Religion* (Maryknoll, NY: Orbis Books, 1994), p. 5.

59. Daniel C. Maguire and Larry L. Rasmussen, *Ethics for a Small Planet: New Horizons on Population, Consumption, and Ecology* (Albany, NY: State University of New York Press, 1998), p. 2.

60. Ibid, p. 3.

61. Ibid.

62. Ibid, p. 15.

63. Ibid, pp. 16–17; italics in original.

64. Daniel C. Maguire and Harold Coward, *Visions of a New Earth: Religious Perspectives on Population, Consumption, and Ecology* (Albany, NY: State University of New York Press, 2000), p. 7.

65. Maguire and Rasmussen, *Ethics,* p. 27.

66. Ibid., p. 41.

67. Ibid., p. 44.

68. Ibid., p. 42.

69. Thomas Berry, *The Great Work: Our Way into the Future* (New York: Bell Tower, 1999), p. 148.

70. Ibid., p. x.

71. Ibid., p. 1.

72. Ibid., p. 115.

73. Ibid., p. 5.

74. Ibid., p. 61.

75. Ibid., p. 161.

76. Ibid., p. 13.

77. Ibid., p. 80.

78. Thomas Berry, *The Dream of the Earth* (San Francisco, CA: Sierra Club Books, 1998), p. 169.

79. Ibid., p. 161.

80. Berry, *Great Work,* p. 18.

81. Berry, *Dream of the Earth,* p. 202.

82. Berry, *Great Work,* p. 19.

83. Ibid., pp. 32–33.

84. Berry, *Dream of the Earth,* p. 16.

85. Berry, *Great Work,* pp. 57–58.

86. Berry, *Dream of the Earth,* p. 91.

87. Ibid., p. 106.

88. Berry, *Great Work,* p. 33.

89. Ibid., p. 24.

90. Ibid., p. 49.

91. Ibid., p. 49–50.

92. Ibid., p. 75.

93. Ibid., p. 78.

94. Ibid., p. 39.
95. Ibid., p. 44.
96. Ibid., p. 26.
97. Ibid., p. 56.
98. Ibid., p. 61.
99. Berry, *Dream of the Earth,* p. 11.
100. Ibid., p. 46.
101. Ibid., p. 81.
102. Ibid., p. 113.
103. Ibid., p. 81.
104. Ibid., pp. xiv–xv.
105. Ibid., p. 223.
106. Ibid., p. 195.
107. John C. Haught, *God after Darwin: A Theology of Evolution* (Boulder, CO: Westview Press, 2000), is his major work on this topic to date.
108. In *God after Darwin,* see particularly chap. 9: "Evolution, Ecology and the Promise of Nature."
109. Ibid., p. 112.
110. Ibid., p. 147.
111. Ibid.
112. Ibid., p. 151.
113. Ibid., p. 152.
114. Ibid., p. 153.
115. Ibid., p. 155.
116. Ibid., p. 159.
117. Ibid.
118. Ibid., p. 160.
119. Ibid., p. 141.

5. Transforming Tradition and Conserving Creation: Southern Visions

1. Marcelo de Barros and José Luis Caravias, *Teología de la Tierra* (Madrid, Spain: Ediciones Paulinas, 1988), p. 11; my translation. I met these authors when we were presenting papers at the "Seminário sobre Teologia da Terra," in Itatiaia, Brazil, January 1989.

2. Ibid., p. 12.

3. Ibid., p. 21.

4. Ibid., p. 23.

5. Ibid., p. 25.

6. Ibid., pp. 25–26.

7. Ibid., p. 35.

8. Ibid., pp. 36–37.

9. Ibid., p. 39.

10. Ibid., p. 75.

11. Ibid., pp. 76–77.

12. Ibid., p. 88.

13. Ibid., p. 90.

14. Ibid., p. 96.

15. Ibid., pp. 101–2.

16. Ibid., p. 118.

17. Ibid., p. 385.

18. Ibid., p. 402.

19. Ibid.

20. Ibid., p. 406.

21. Ibid., p. 411.

22. Ibid., p. 412.

23. Ibid., p. 420.

24. Ibid.

25. Ibid., p. 422.

26. Ibid., p. 427.

27. Ibid., p. 428.

28. Ibid., p. 429.

29. Marcelo de Barros, "A Pastoral da Terra e o Desafio da Espiritualidade," in *A Teologia se Fez Terra,* p. 110. My translation. The book is the published version of selected papers from the conference, with a foreword by Bishop Pedro Casaldáliga and an introduction by conference organizer Alfredo Ferro Medina, S.J. The papers include my own presentation, "Para um Jubileu Novo."

30. De Barros, "Pastoral, " p. 113.

31. Ibid., p. 117.

32. Leonardo Boff, *Ecology and Liberation: A New Paradigm* (Maryknoll, NY: Orbis Books, 1996), p. 7.

33. Ibid., p. 15.

34. Ibid., p. 18.

35. Ibid., pp. 21, 23, 25.

36. Ibid., p. 27.

37. Ibid., p. 30.

38. Leonardo Boff, *Cry of the Earth, Cry of the Poor* (Maryknoll, NY: Orbis Books, 1997), p. 133.

39. Ibid., pp. 112, 131.

40. Boff, *Ecology,* p. 88.

41. Ibid., p. 46.

42. Ibid., pp. 49, 51.

43. Ibid., p. 43.

44. Ibid., p. 65.

45. Ibid., p. 148.

46. Boff, *Cry of the Earth,* p. xi.

47. Ibid., p. 1.

48. Ibid., p. 5.

49. Ibid., p. 132.

50. Ibid., p. 13.

51. Ibid., pp. 28, 40, 50.

52. Ibid., pp. 29, 32.

53. Ibid., pp. 115, 116.

54. Ibid., p. 118.

55. Ibid., p. 81.

56. Ibid., p. 37.

57. Ibid., p. 83.

58. Ibid., p. 167.

59. Ibid., p. 185.

60. Ibid., p. 183.

61. Ibid., p. 199.

62. Ibid., pp. 119, 122.

63. Ibid., p. 117.

64. Ibid., p. 112.

65. Ibid., pp. 142, 147–48.

66. Ibid., p. 151.

67. "Ivone Gebara," in Mev Puleo, ed., *The Struggle Is One: Voices and Visions of Liberation* (Albany, NY: State University of New York Press, 1994), pp. 208, 209, 214, 215, 216.

68. Ivone Gebara, *Longing for Running Water: Ecofeminism and Liberation* (Minneapolis, MN: Fortress Press, 1999), p. vi.

69. Ibid., p. vii.

70. Ibid., p. 1.

71. Ibid., p. 3.

72. Ibid.

73. Ibid., pp. 4–5.

74. Ibid., p. 8.

75. Ibid., p. 17.

76. Ibid., pp. 50, 51.

77. Ibid., pp. 52, 53.

78. Ibid., p. 64.

79. Ibid., p. 67.

80. Ibid., p. 80.

81. Ibid., p. 97.

82. Ibid., p. 99.

83. Ibid., p. 115.

84. Ibid., p. 81.

85. Ibid., p. 83.

86. Ibid., p. 87.

87. Ibid., p. 131.

88. Ibid., p. 183.

6. Creation Consciousness and Concern

1. James H. Cone, "Whose Earth Is It, Anyway?" in Dieter Hessel and Larry Rasmussen, eds., *Earth Habitat: Eco-Injustice and the Church's Response* (Minneapolis, MN: Fortress Press, 2001), pp. 23–32.

2. Ibid., p. 23.

3. Ibid., p. 26.

4. Ibid., p. 27.

5. The *Earth Charter* has been made available, free of charge to download and print, at www.earthcharter.org.

6. This telegram is in the headquarters of Green Cross International, Geneva, Switzerland; a copy was provided to this author by Sabine Arrobbio of Green Cross International.

7. Care for Creation and Community

1. These representative projects and similar ones are described on the USCC Web site, Department of Social Development and World Peace, Environmental Justice Program (www.nccbuscc.org/sdwp/ejp).

Selected Bibliography

Berry, Thomas. *The Dream of the Earth.* San Francisco, CA: Sierra Club Books, 1988.

————. *The Great Work: Our Way into the Future.* New York: Bell Tower, 1999.

Berry, Wendell. (Norman Wirzba, ed.) *The Art of the Commonplace: The Agrarian Essays of Wendell Berry.* New York: Basic Books, 2002.

————. *Life Is a Miracle: An Essay against Modern Superstition.* Washington, DC: Counterpoint, 2000.

————. *The Gift of Good Land: Further Essays, Cultural and Agricultural.* San Francisco, CA: North Point Press, 1981.

————. *The Unsettling of America: Culture and Agriculture.* New York: Avon Books, 1978.

Black Elk. *The Sacred Pipe: Black Elk's Account of the Seven Rites of the Oglala Sioux.* Recorded and edited by Joseph Epes Brown. New York: Penguin Books, 1976.

Boff, Leonardo. *Cry of the Earth, Cry of the Poor.* Maryknoll, NY: Orbis Books, 1997.

————. *Ecology and Liberation: A New Paradigm.* Maryknoll, NY: Orbis Books, 1996.

Brown, Joseph Epes. *The Spiritual Legacy of the American Indian.* New York: Crossroad, 1982.

Christiansen, Drew, S.J., and Walter Grazer, eds. *"And God Saw That It Was Good": Catholic Theology and the Environment.* Washington, DC: United States Catholic Conference, 1996.

159

De Barros, Marcelo, and José Luis Caravias. *Teología de la Tierra.* Madrid, Spain: Ediciones Paulinas, 1988. Simultaneous publication: *Teologia da Terra.* Petrópolis, Brazil: Editora Vozes Ltda., 1988.

DeMallie, Raymond J. *The Sixth Grandfather: Black Elk's Teachings Given to John G. Neihardt.* Lincoln, NE: University of Nebraska Press, 1985.

Engel, J. Ronald. *Sacred Sands: The Struggle for Community in the Indiana Dunes.* Middletown, CT: Wesleyan University Press, 1983.

Evans, Bernard F., and Gregory D. Cusack. *Theology of the Land.* Collegeville, MN: The Liturgical Press, 1987.

Ferro Medina, Alfredo, S.J., ed. *A Teologia se Fez Terra: Primeiro Encontro Latino-Americano de Teologia da Terra.* São Leopoldo, Brasil: Editora Sinodal, 1991.

Fox, Matthew. *Creation Spirituality: Liberating Gifts for the Peoples of the Earth.* San Francisco, CA: HarperSanFrancisco, 1991.

————. *Original Blessing: A Primer in Creation Spirituality.* Santa Fe, NM: Bear & Co., 1986.

Gebara, Ivone. *Longing for Running Water: Ecofeminism and Liberation.* Minneapolis, MN: Fortress Press, 1999.

Grim, John A., ed. *Indigenous Traditions and Ecology: The Interbeing of Cosmology and Community.* Cambridge, MA: Harvard University Press, 2001.

Hart, John. *Ethics and Technology: Innovation and Transformation in Community Contexts.* Cleveland, OH: The Pilgrim Press, 1997.

————. "A Jubilee for a New Millennium: Justice for the Earth and for Peoples of the Land," *Catholic Rural Life,* Vol. 43: No. 2, Spring 2001.

————. *The Spirit of the Earth: A Theology of the Land.* Mahwah, NJ: Paulist Press, 1984.

Haught, John F. *God after Darwin: A Theology of Evolution.* Boulder, CO: Westview Press, 2000.

————. "Information and Cosmic Purpose." John F. Haught, ed., *Science and Religion in Search of Cosmic Purpose.* Washington, DC: Georgetown University Press, 2000.

Hessel, Dieter, and Larry Rasmussen, eds. *Earth Habitat: Eco-Injustice and the Church's Response.* Minneapolis, MN: Fortress Press, 2001.

Hessel, Dieter T., and Rosemary Radford Ruether, eds. *Christianity and Ecology: Seeking the Well-Being of Earth and Humans*. *Cambridge,* MA: Harvard University Press, 2000.

Jackson, Wes. *Altars of Unhewn Stone: Science and the Earth*. San Francisco, CA: North Point Press, 1987.

————. *Becoming Native to This Place*. Lexington, KY: The University Press of Kentucky, 1994.

John Paul II. *The Ecological Crisis: A Common Responsibility*. Washington, DC: United States Catholic Conference, 1990.

King, Paul G., and David O. Woodward. *Liberating Nature: Theology and Economics in a New World Order*. Cleveland, OH: The Pilgrim Press, 1999.

Kinsley, David. *Theology and Religion: Ecological Spirituality in Cross-Cultural Perspective*. Englewood Cliffs, NJ: Prentice-Hall, 1995.

Leopold, Aldo. *A Sand County Almanac—And Sketches Here and There*. New York: Oxford University Press, 1987.

Maguire, Daniel C., and Harold Coward. *Visions of a New Earth: Religious Perspectives on Population, Consumption, and Ecology*. Albany, NY: State University of New York Press, 2000.

Maguire, Daniel C., and Larry L. Rasmussen. *Ethics for a Small Planet: New Horizons on Population, Consumption, and Ecology*. Albany, NY: State University of New York Press, 1998.

Mails, Thomas E. *Fools Crow*. New York: Avon Books, 1980.

McGrath, Alistair. *The Reenchantment of Nature—The Denial of Religion and the Ecological Crisis*. New York: Doubleday, 2002.

Nash, James A. *Loving Nature: Ecological Integrity and Christian Responsibility*. Nashville, TN: Abingdon Press, 1992.

Nash, Roderick Frazier. *The Rights of Nature: A History of Environmental Ethics*. Madison, WI: The University of Wisconsin Press, 1989.

Neihardt, John G. *Black Elk Speaks: Being the Life Story of a Holy Man of the Oglala Sioux*. New York: Pocket Books, 1972.

Puleo, Mev. *The Struggle Is One: Voices and Visions of Liberation*. Albany, NY: State University of New York Press, 1994.

Rasmussen, Larry L. *Earth Community Earth Ethics*. Maryknoll, NY: Orbis Books, 1996.

Rolston, Holmes, III. *Conserving Natural Value.* New York: Columbia University Press, 1994.

Ruether, Rosemary Radford. *Gaia and God: An Ecofeminist Theology of Earth Healing.* San Francisco, CA: HarperSanFrancisco, 1994.

————, ed. *Women Healing Earth: Third World Women on Ecology, Feminism, and Religion.* Maryknoll, NY: Orbis Books, 1994.

Smith, Pamela. *What Are They Saying about Environmental Ethics?* Mahwah, NJ: Paulist Press, 1997.

Swimme, Brian, and Thomas Berry. *The Universe Story: From the Primordial Flaring Forth to the Ecozoic Era—A Celebration of the Unfolding of the Cosmos.* San Francisco, CA: HarperSanFrancisco, 1992.

U.S. Catholic Bishops. *Global Climate Change: A Plea for Dialogue, Prudence and the Common Good.* Washington, DC: United States Catholic Conference, 2001.

————. *Renewing the Earth: An Invitation to Reflection and Action on Environment in Light of Catholic Social Teaching.* Washington, DC: United States Catholic Conference, 1991.

Index

Other Books in This Series

Other Books in This Series